NEW CORPORATE VENTURES

NEW CORPORATE VENTURES

How to Make Them Work

Ralph Alterowitz
with
Jon Zonderman

WILEY

JOHN WILEY & SONS
New York • Chichester • Brisbane • Toronto • Singapore

This publication is designed to provide accurate and
authoritative information in regard to the subject
matter covered. It is sold with the understanding that
the publisher is not engaged in rendering legal, accounting,
or other professional service. If legal advice or other
expert assistance is required, the services of a competent
professional person should be sought. *From a Declaration
of Principles jointly adopted by a Committee of the
American Bar Association and a Committee of Publishers.*

Library of Congress Cataloging in Publication Data:

Alterowitz, Ralph.
  New corporate ventures : how to make them work / by Ralph
Alterowitz with Jon Zonderman.
    p. cm.
  ISBN 0-471-62418-7
    1. Industrial management—United States. 2. Venture capital—
United States. 3. New business enterprises—United States—
Management. 4. Entrepreneurship—United States. I. Zonderman,
Jon. II. Title.
HD70.U5A414 1988
658.1'1—dc19   87-34925
                                                                  CIP

Printed in the United States of America

10 9 8 7 6 5 4 3 2 1

PREFACE

Entrepreneurship has been the key factor in the continuing renewal of American business. Entrepreneurial creativity has led to new ventures, which in turn have harnessed the entrepreneurial energy of individuals—in the long run continually reshaping and revitalizing the American economy.

But large corporations have generally been unsuccessful at planned renewal. Management orientation, direction of resources, and measurement of success are focused on near-term results.

Coupled with the less than flexible corporate culture, this leads to the key reasons existing corporations have found it difficult to be entrepreneurial. And as small companies grow, they develop and acquire the trappings of mature companies that make being innovative and entrepreneurial difficult.

Corporate executives have internalized a mode of behavior that is anathema to successful venturing. They are too blinded by the pressures of running ongoing businesses to see the special needs of new, immature business ventures, and have tried to impose the same kind of management on ventures that is successful in running ongoing businesses.

Too often, badly conceived and badly managed attempts

at corporate venturing lead to waste of a business's three most precious resources: people, money, and time. Perhaps the greatest waste is in human resources, in a loss of human incentive, emotional commitment to the enterprise, and potential.

This book is intended to show corporate executives a way of conducting internal corporate ventures that will increase the possibility of success. It presents a three-part argument:

- Corporate venturing must be done in order to continue the American business tradition of renewal and entrepreneurship.
- If it is done right, resources can be used effectively, and people will be motivated and enthusiastic rather than drained or embittered by the experience.
- In order to do venturing correctly, corporate executives must think of ventures as a species of business different from the ongoing businesses of the company.

The book also seeks to help corporations develop and maintain better working relationships with corporate entrepreneurs. Many authors and lecturers have focused on getting ideas generated within the corporation, assuming this would develop corporate entrepreneurs.

But entrepreneurs do not need to be developed; they are waiting to show what they can do. They merely need to be identified and nurtured. Then they and their ideas need to be integrated into the fabric of the corporation as seamlessly as possible. In order to do this, corporate executives need to keep in mind some fundamental points.

Although ideas come from individuals, it is the corporation that develops those ideas. This means that in corporate venturing the corporation assumes a much larger share of the risk than an investor in an independent venture. Because of this, if the corporation is not committed to taking the initiative—and the risk—it should not get involved.

The origin of this book goes back nearly a decade. In 1979, the manager of new business development for IBM asked me to develop a better approach for screening and evaluating the company's new ventures. The goal was to improve the success rate, which at that time was as dismal as most corporations'—on the order of 10–20 percent.

I presented my findings to IBM a short time later, but have continued to study the problem since then. This book represents the results of my continued effort, which are my own work and, I must point out, in no way reflect the official thinking of IBM.

One thing I found while doing research on the then-current screening and evaluation process was that, ironically, despite a long "corporate memory" for most things, that memory was short when it came to the experiences and lessons learned in trying to start new ventures.

What I have found is that there is a specific process for developing new ventures, of which screening and evaluation is only one part. Success depends far more on such things as the "corporate culture," the "follow-through," and the capability of the evaluator, than on screening and evaluation techniques.

The process begins before screening and ends when the product or business dies. Maintaining the integrity of the process—following through from one phase to the next—is critical to preventing major mistakes and minimizing serious losses.

In order to develop a model process for corporate venturing, I turned to those with the most successful approach to venturing—venture capitalists. Their operations provided most of the data needed to describe and understand the dynamics of venturing. Venture capital operations are ideal for analysis because they are not complicated by the political, organizational, and cultural considerations that impinge on any issue being studied in companies.

From this examination I distilled the essence of the venturing process. Creating a generic process offers a way for companies to take the lessons of venture capital and build them into a corporate framework. The argument was never to have corporations mimic venture capital completely. That, as we all know, would be impossible because of the corporate structures and pressures.

What the venture capital model affords corporations is a way to organize the venturing effort into a continuous process, to use information about past ventures—both successes and failures—to build a data base of experience on which the next venture can be built. In this way, I hope to help companies get away from the conventional, haphazard approach to new business development, where one or more failures are evaluated, individual problems in the failures are identified, and "quick-fix" solutions are offered so the same problems do not crop up again next time.

The current concern for improving U.S. competitiveness and improving corporate performance is certainly one driving force for improving the corporate venturing success rate. Another, and possibly larger concern, however, should be the damage to individuals caused by failed ventures.

Rarely do executives and others involved in failed corporate ventures think of the lost opportunities, the dashed hopes, the disappointments, and the drop in morale that affect everyone involved in the ventures.

For many people associated with the venture, failure means they will not realize their personal objectives of expressing their creativity, showing their initiative, or demonstrating their skills. They have bought into the venture's promises and possibly even been "bitten by the entrepreneurial bug," only to see their hopes dashed.

Most executives, however, feel that personnel in the venture are working on one of many possible assignments in the company. They take their chance along with everyone else on any project in the company. While that is true, the pain is much harder to handle when the venture fails because of poor and inadequate management than when a technological breakthrough does not happen or the product fails in the marketplace. Rekindling the spirit many people brought to the venture is hard. The loss in human commitment and the economic loss are certainly sufficient to warrant doing something about venturing.

This book does not pretend to present a magical solution for success. The guidance offered increases the work involved in starting new ventures in companies. To do it right and well demands commitment: deciding to do it, making the major changes, and implementing the process. Companies must be prepared to face the challenges caused by newness and by having to follow a process that is just as demanding as the one for running the ongoing business.

RALPH ALTEROWITZ

Potomac, MD
April 1988

ACKNOWLEDGMENTS

In my case, as with any author, many people have been a part of this book, by contributing to the development and refinement of the idea, and by providing information.

Much is owed to Abraham Katz, IBM's former director of planning systems, who was my mentor. He espoused the systems and process approach to business operations. Over the years, I have become increasingly indebted to my long-time associate and close friend Richard A. Leshuk for his many insights into contemporary industry practices.

Albert Rubenstein, the Walter P. Murphy Professor at Northwestern University's Technological Institute, kept searching for the "fatal flaws" in both the concept and structure of the book.

Several people are directly responsible for the book. Daan van Alderwerelt, as the IBM manager of new business development, posed the starting request—to develop a better approach for evaluating new ventures—and supported the effort. For the last three years I have had the good fortune to work for Richard V. Bergstresser, the director of the IBM scientific centers, who gave me the opportunity to continue the work and encouraged me to write the book.

Venture capitalists provided valuable and necessary in-

Acknowledgments

sights and contributed operational and anecdotal information so that a model process could be synthesized. Their support, openness, warmth, and caring left as much of a permanent mark on me as the information they shared.

I will never forget the exchanges with William A. Draper, III; Tommy J. Davis; Reid J. Dennis; Stanley C. Golder; Robert Zicarelli; James R. Swartz; H. Dubose Montgomery; John R. Dougery; Henry L. B. Wilder; Pedro Castillo; Dr. Ralph Biggadike; Ben Kilgore; John W. Pearson; Dr. James Tait Elder; Karen Davis; Donald T. Valentine; E. F. Heizer, Jr.; Daniel T. Kingsley; and the ongoing dialogues with Lucien Ruby and Pete Linsert. And thanks to the many others who have directly and indirectly contributed to the book.

For the direction, prodding, patience, and commitment to make the book see the light of day, I owe Jon Zonderman. Jon's writing skill and support made this book more like a labor of love than the torture it could have been. John Mahaney guided and then painstakingly edited the book at John Wiley and Sons; Helen Rees, my agent, shepherded the project from conception to final product.

And from the beginning until the end, I would be nowhere without my research associate, editor, harshest critic, strongest supporter, dearest love, and wonderful wife. She worked with me on the previous effort, which led to the New Business Venturism monograph, and is as much a part of this book as I am.

R. A.

CONTENTS

Contents

NEW CORPORATE VENTURES

Introduction

Internal Corporate Venturing: Is It Worth the Effort?

Everyone knows who Steve Jobs is, but few people know who Paul Friedl is. Everyone remembers the Apple II, but who has ever heard of the SCAMP? Steve Jobs and Steve Wozniak changed the way business operates and people live. Paul Friedl came up with a good product, the world's first PC.

The SCAMP prototype Friedl demonstrated to John Opel, president of IBM, on a rainy September evening in Atlanta in 1973 was reported by the *Wall Street Journal* as the world's first portable computer when IBM announced it as the 5100 less than a year later. No one thought of the 5100 as a personal computer, yet its portability and "personability" were demonstrated by the fact that 5100s were "walking out the door" in employees' arms. Customer complaints of thefts made IBM redesign the machine into the 5120.

Between the 5100 and the time the IBM PC was announced in late 1982, the company had already gone through two other PC-related efforts. The PC was the third in a series of announced products. Although the first and second products were successful in that they met or exceeded sales forecasts, they did not redirect the computer industry and start the new wave.

Clearly, as far as IBM was concerned, the PC was an innovative product. But its success begs two questions: Having had the technical lead and a tangible product in 1973, why did IBM have to wait until its fourth try to achieve success? And why did a small company like Apple achieve the success that was literally in IBM's hands years before?

In this case, the answer for the large corporation is not in the product or the technology, but in the organizational structure and the perception of starting a new business. The fourth attempt was truly handled as a new venture, in that it was directed by an organization within IBM set up specifically to create a new product.

In January 1973, when Friedl was asked to develop a portable computer that used the APL programming language, he was told that he would have all the resources he needed. In 1976, what began as the computer-in-the-home (CITH) effort was also given resources, but other parts of the home-entertainment project ran into technical difficulties. When the total project was dissolved, the CITH prototype was transferred to IBM's Boca Raton, Florida, facility. Shortly afterward the effort was cancelled so that the resources could be applied to developing a small computer for business applications, the 8100.

In 1980, IBM initiated its venturing program. The company decided that "independent business units" (IBUs) would be set up to develop worthwhile ideas into businesses. The project of developing the IBM PC became one of these IBUs. The IBUs were free of the routine administration, bureaucracy, planning, and operating constraints of other operating units.

By 1982, IBM had 15 IBUs exploring opportunities and developing ventures in a number of different product and market areas. They were "incubators" for start-up businesses that were supposed to nurture the new business until it succeeded and could be integrated into the IBM superstructure.

DIFFICULTIES OF VENTURING

Even the largest and most successful companies have a terribly difficult time starting new ventures. Ventures involve a high degree of innovation—traveling far from the company's core business in terms of either product, or market, or both.

Venture capitalists, who make a living by funding innovative businesses, have said that they succeed better than half the time. Data supports their contention. Even more significant is that they receive a return on at least 80 percent of the money they invest.

Entrepreneurs, those who develop the venture ideas and often manage these innovative new businesses, succeed about 20 percent of the time on their first try. The probability of success doubles to 40 percent on their next attempt. These statistics suggest that once an entrepreneur becomes successful, future successes are that much easier to come by.

The same, unfortunately, is not true for corporations. By their own admission, corporations are stuck with a success rate of between 10 and 20 percent, both for ventures and for return on money invested. They are often successful at product extensions and at finding new applications for existing products. But rarely are they able to move very far from their core business, or to extend both the market and product to the point where the new business can be considered truly innovative.

WHAT IS VENTURING?

When people think of venturing, they often think of venture capitalists and independent entrepreneurs. But established companies are increasingly entering the world of venturing, either by setting up venture-capital pools to invest in outside ventures or by creating ventures internally.

In the context of the corporation, an internal venture takes the company beyond its core business—the set of products and services and markets that provide the company's income. Our illustration shows this using IBM in the early 1980s as an example. Diverging from the core business means finding new applications, products, or markets. In many cases, the core technology—the underlying skills, proprietary techniques, and know-how—will be the foundation for all new efforts.

Computers, copiers, and related products for business and government were IBM's core in the late 1970s. IBM venturing efforts at this time included efforts to develop both new products for existing markets and new products for new markets. Some of the more notable of these included:

• Satellite Business Systems, a joint venture since sold to MCI, provided microwave communication services

IBM New Business Activity

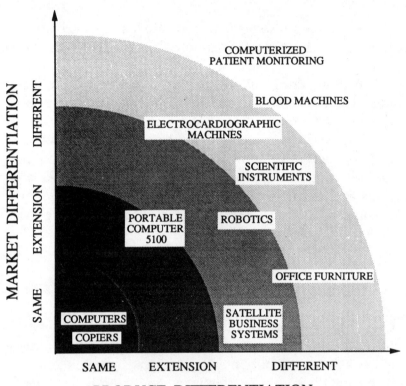

for voice and data to the company's existing business market.

- An office furniture start-up that addressed the needs of existing customers of data-processing equipment.
- Biomedical Systems, with two product lines, blood-processing equipment and electrocardiograph machines. Both were sold to new markets: laboratories, doctors, and hospitals.

• IBM Instruments began marketing a new set of products to scientific laboratories.

The company also made a foray into home entertainment systems, with products it spun off into DiscoVision Associates.

Venturing does not necessarily mean that a company must use new technology. The technology may be new to the company, but well-developed in other companies. In extreme cases, a company will acquire or undertake new technological development that could be the underpinning for new businesses. In these examples, IBM used core skills and technology such as data processing, signal processing and analysis, data storage, printing technology, and data communications.

WHY VENTURING?

One of the reasons for the high mortality rate of new ventures in companies is that executives are not clear on their reasons for developing new businesses. Independent venture capitalists say that this is evident even in their dealings with corporate venture-capital organizations, which should have similar financial objectives as independent venturists. The lack of clear corporate objectives is responsible, in great part, for the independent venture capitalists' reluctance to co-invest with corporations.

This is also a problem for those who develop new businesses within corporations. The confusion over balancing new business goals with traditional financial objectives causes vacillation, ambivalence, redirection, and project cancellation. Executives who believe a project is a mistake often have the power to overrule new-business professionals. New-business efforts in large companies are often turned down because the revenue outlook for most new businesses is analogous to a flea on an elephant.

Valid reasons for getting involved in any new business— whether created internally or acquired—include gaining a window on technology, company growth, and the potential return on investment. The technology window can materialize in the short term if a company is serious and sensitive to developments in the field. But growth usually will not be evident for at least three to five years, and a return on investment may not be seen for eight years or more. Although venture professionals know that these are the facts of investment life, corporate executives often get disheartened.

Unfortunately the most common reason companies get into new ventures is what we call the "last-chance syndrome" or "panic diversification." This unstated but underlying reason for new-business development is often brought on by declining sales of the company's existing product line with no follow-on products, and it can push the company into acquisitions and hastily conceived product extensions. Larger companies are less likely to experience this effect because they sell a variety of products. However, single-product divisions of large corporations as well as small companies may find themselves in this situation.

VENTURE BEFORE IT IS NECESSARY

Internal venturing can be a very good protective device for countering future threats to a company's products, technologies, and markets. While real growth may not occur for years, new-business activity provides the perception of renewal, with all the positive effects.

Personnel become motivated by the perception of opportunity for promotion, a broader range of applications for their skills, and the economic promise offered by a company that is expanding. New ventures enable companies to employ surplus capacity, capture people potential, and retain key personnel. Investors also infer growth from new-product development.

New business also has a positive effect on the mainline business and the company climate. Internal venturing produces a continuing pressure on management to think in strategic terms and increases the sensitivity to new developments in the market. Entering new businesses in a planned way—planned venturing—tends to preclude "hardening of the arteries," especially in long-established companies in traditional industries, and it is the key to continuing renewal of the corporation. Many companies, however, enter venturing in an ad-hoc way because they think they should do something, but they don't know what.

The message is short, but powerful. Companies need entrepreneurial activity. Corporate entrepreneurs provide a stimulus to the entire company.

But companies must have the right climate to fully utilize their people potential. The growth of the venture-capital industry and the "instant millionaires" it has created enticed many creative and entrepreneurial people to leave companies, taking their skills, knowledge, and even other people with them. This growth has increased competition and raised the price tag for good ideas and good deals.

Companies can lose in two ways: they lose the technical and creative talent, and they lose management expertise. Venture capitalists rarely fund a single entrepreneur or in-

Role of New Business Activity

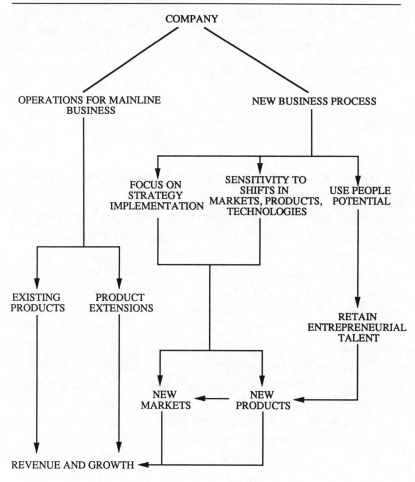

ventor. They fund entrepreneurial teams: technical, marketing, and management.

In the long run, the people holding the potential for their companies' futures are the ones most likely to leave. Corporate executives who claim that the number of people leaving is small miss the point. It is not the number that is important, but rather the quality of people and the number of ideas lost.

THE SUCCESSFUL CORPORATE VENTURE PROGRAM

The fact that most corporate ventures fail is evidence of substantial problems that afflict almost all companies and their ventures. We will define these problems closely.

Because these problems are systemic, any good solution to corporate venturing problems must be capable of addressing the entire business of venturing. Too often companies believe they can correct problems in venturing with a quick fix.

The new-venture business must be conceived of and designed as an integrated system to carry out the objective of spawning successful new ventures.

My solution is generic and therefore applicable to all companies, but permits customizing in its implementation. It takes into consideration the special challenges created by the corporate setting. I do not seek to have corporations change their basic way of doing business. I ask only that corporations treat ventures differently from the way they treat ongoing business.

Corporate new ventures are part of a particular, established company, which has a culture, operating style, and vested interests, and is concerned about exposures, threats, and liability. The new-venture business management and the corporate management must be concerned with relationships: between the corporation and the new-venture business, company personnel and the new-venture business personnel, the corporation and each new venture, and the corporation and each corporate entrepreneur.

The following chapters take the reader through a step-by-step discussion of the process of successfully establishing an internal venturing mechanism that increases the probability of success and is consistent with corporate goals.

Chapter 1 identifies the five major problem areas of corporation venturing, and establishes the basis for developing a comprehensive and consistent solution.

Chapter 2 deals with the new-venture process, the sequence of phases that must be executed in order to transform an idea into a business.

Chapter 3 looks at screening and evaluation, the stages of refinement an idea passes through on its way to being developed into a business.

Chapter 4 explains the need for, and preparation of, a business plan, the first step in articulating an idea and the basis for an evaluation of the proposal.

Chapter 5 examines the new-venture charter, or "contract," that the corporate management must make with those who will run its new-venture business and, in effect, with itself. How will its internal venturing effort be conducted?

Chapter 6 compares the different operating styles and cultures of ongoing businesses and new ventures, and examines how to prepare the ongoing business for the introduction of new ventures. The "venture shock" that corporate cultures often undergo in the midst of a corporate venturing program is described and analyzed.

Chapter 7 discusses the problems of identifying and motivating corporate entrepreneurs, and of getting them interested in the corporate venturing program.

Chapter 8 examines four organizational options for a corporation's internal venture effort.

Chapter 9 looks at issues involved in staffing both the corporate venturing effort and each individual venture.

Chapter 10 deals with the ultimate measure of a company's commitment to venturing—funding. The options for funding the new-venture effort and individual ventures are inextricably linked with the organizational options discussed in Chapter 8.

Chapter 11 tackles perhaps the most difficult part of the venturing process, the close monitoring and nurturing that must take place during the first few years of a venture's existence, as well as the intricacies of "divesting" of a venture, often by transferring it during its "adolescence" into the mainstream of the corporation's ongoing business.

Chapter One

Corporate Venturing Problems

John Rockwell, former president of Booz-Allen Venture Management, comes closest to articulating the reasons for the reality of poor corporate venturing when he notes that companies approach the new-product process as "a sequential problem" rather than as part of an integrated dynamic process.

A number of studies have analyzed the reasons for the failure of corporations in establishing truly innovative businesses. The array of reasons cited covers almost anything and everything that could go wrong, but blame is most commonly placed on

- Defective product
- Inadequate market analysis
- Insufficient marketing effort
- Higher costs than expected
- Poor timing
- Technical obsolescence
- Poor management
- Problems inherent in the market

• Conflicts with laws and regulations
• Insufficient capital
• Problems with the technology

These problems are found from company to company and across diverse industries. This is hardly coincidental; rather it points to the fact that there is something fundamentally wrong with the way venturing is undertaken by companies with successful ongoing businesses.

A study by Booz-Allen & Hamilton suggests that most companies that initiated new businesses had difficulties in seven fundamental areas.* Figure 1-1 shows some of Booz-Allen's results. Eighty-one percent of the companies had difficulties with organization, 35 percent had problems with control and follow-up, 26 percent with the definition of objectives, and 26 percent with business analysis. New ideas and creativity, personnel qualifications, and performance of steps in the process were also recorded as recurring problems.

In further analysis (Figure 1-2), Booz-Allen showed that the area of "organization," which was identified as the major problem, really consisted of many parts, including structures and procedures, the definition of responsibilities, difficulties in working and reporting relationships, communications, and top-management support. Confusion as to responsibilities creates obstacles in working and reporting relationships and in communications.

The point is that there are basic problems associated with running any venture that are separate from the particular risks associated with getting into any specific new

---

* "Management of the New Product," Booz-Allen & Hamilton Inc., 1968.

Figure 1-1. New Business Problem Areas

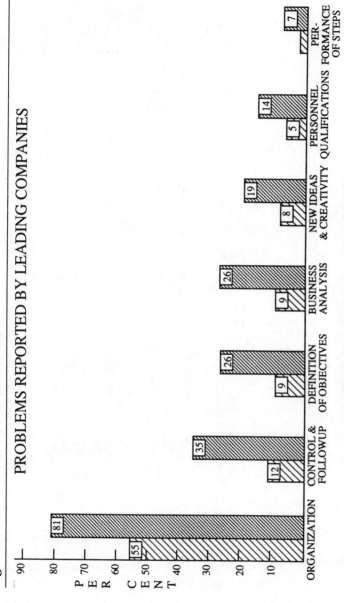

PROBLEMS REPORTED BY LEADING COMPANIES

PERCENT OF COMPANIES REPORTING PROBLEM
PERCENT OF PROBLEMS REPORTED

Source: BOOZ-ALLEN & HAMILTON, reprinted by permission.

• 15 •

Figure 1-2. Organization Problems

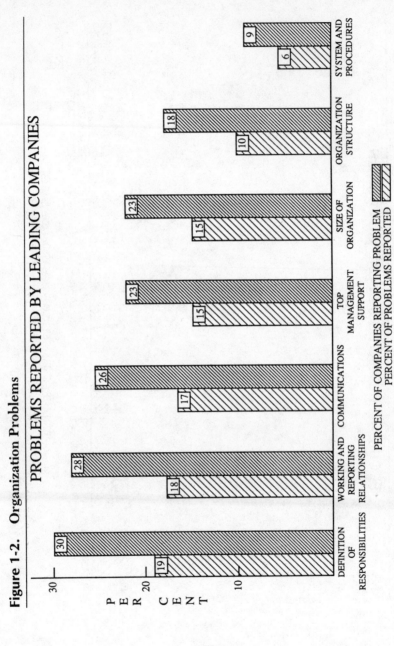

PROBLEMS REPORTED BY LEADING COMPANIES

Source: BOOZ-ALLEN & HAMILTON, reprinted by permission

business. Some of the business risks may be minimized if the generic venturing problems are dealt with.

Many analysts, both in large-scale studies and in post-mortem analyses of a particular venture for a company, focus on the risks of the particular business when trying to determine why a venture has failed. Because of the lack of attention to the generic venturing problems, most companies will continue to fail time after time when it comes to establishing new ventures.

The compartmentalized approach to running an ongoing business, when transplanted to the operation of a new venture, points out one of the central flaws in the way companies think of new businesses.

Too many executives think of new businesses in the same way they think of their ongoing businesses. These executives think the new business can be run like the ongoing company, and that it *should* be run like the ongoing company; that the structure will be similar, that control mechanisms, objectives, ways of analyzing success, and other factors will all be similar. At the very least they believe that, despite the obvious differences, new ventures can function within the structure of the existing business.

New-business development is different from running an ongoing business. Figure 1-3 (see page 30) shows how the operational characteristics of a new business differ from those of an ongoing business. Equally important, the inception, development, and nurturing of new ventures are much different from running an existing business.

The following five problem areas are most responsible for new-business failure:

• Lack of direction and strategy
• Unrealistic management expectations

- Ignorance of the venturing process
- Transfer problems
- Culture conflict

These problems affect every aspect of business: people, organization, and management. They point to the need for an all-encompassing solution, not one that is piecemeal or just a quick fix.

LACK OF DIRECTION AND STRATEGY

Top management must write meaningful objectives for new-business development, to guide both the professionals who will be searching for and developing ventures and the line managers who will eventually be running those ventures. These objectives must go beyond generalities to specify the technology of interest and define the nature of the corporation's desired presence in the industry.

Line managers may reject a good idea because they don't recognize its value. Their negative reaction also sets the stage for future contributions from their personnel: a lackluster reception by a manager who does not know what to do with an idea will reduce the employee's eagerness to submit new ideas in the future.

The lack of a strategy denies direction and constraints to those who will actually find, develop, and manage new ventures. Venture professionals and managers need guidelines for evaluating new ideas. Without a document that sets forth the objectives and the strategy for achieving the objectives, and without available resources properly allocated, there can be no basis for deciding which ideas are worth looking at in greater detail. Without some sort of written direction, criteria can be derived only from anecdotal management comments and will lack the consistency and compatibility provided by a carefully planned and articulated strategy.

UNREALISTIC MANAGEMENT EXPECTATIONS

Too often unrealistic expectations prevail in such areas as

- Ease of getting started
- The number of ideas that make business sense
- Timing
- Financial return

Many seasoned managers don't realize that development of new ventures is far different from running an established business.

A former vice-president of marketing was part of the management team in a new-venture offering of a high-tech medical product. His solution to poor sales was to hire more people to sell, never contacting the prospective customer group. Even when the venture went under, he never thought of revamping his promotion and marketing plans and never understood why the product didn't sell. In his previous position as a marketing executive for a large corporation, he had not dealt with such problems directly, and when faced with an unfamiliar challenge, he did not know how to handle it.

Of the many expectations that cause problems for the new-venture business, two of the most damaging are the belief that "we have plenty of good ideas around and all we need to do is to start doing something about them," and the demand that "we want to see profits in two years." It is impossible to program when good ideas will be brought forward. Flexibility is a must, and a venturing program must be long-term.

Companies are not discriminating enough in their initial selection of ideas. They evaluate too many ideas thoroughly, and spend money developing too many "dogs." The best proof of this comes from a Booz-Allen & Hamilton survey of 51 companies, which showed that of all the ideas received, more than 50 percent were evaluated to some degree and 25 percent went into development. Ultimately, only 2 percent reached the market, a bad performance. To have only 2 percent of the ideas reach the market is not unusual. What made this a bad performance was that 48 percent of the ideas were evaluated in some depth and then dropped. Unless many more ideas are sifted out of the system earlier, the consideration of new ventures becomes prohibitively expensive.

Contrast this with research by one of the innovation centers funded by the National Science Foundation. The Oregon Innovation Center found that only 5 to 10 percent of ideas proposed were worth evaluating. Most ideas submitted are not suitable for new businesses, and negligible effort is needed to separate those few that are workable from the many that are not.

Analysis of information provided by 11 of the most successful venture-capital firms confirms commercialization of no more than 2 percent of all ideas. But this 2 percent represented *almost all* ideas that were funded for development. The successful firms evaluated fewer than 25 percent of all ideas they received in depth.

Too many companies consider too many ventures because of haste. They say: let's find a venture in the next few months and set up a budget. Although a corporation may have an abundance of ideas, none of them may be right for investment. But pressure from top management, which abhors delays, may prompt investments in poor ventures, ultimately contributing to management's bias that the program is not worthwhile and jeopardizing future management support.

The other big problem is financial expectations. Once an investment is made, management is impatient for results. New businesses rarely do well in the first few years, despite the desires of all involved.

Executives in one company told the manager of a new business that he was expected to produce profits in two years because the venture was already three years old. But in the same three years, the venture had already had two chief executives. The third, on whom the burden was placed, was in the midst of resetting all calibrations, objectives, and targets, thereby reducing the momentum just as his predecessor had. Not only did he have the problem of picking up the pieces of previous managements and not knowing anything about the business area, but he was fighting the laws of probability that say it is rare for any corporate venture to be profitable in two years.

According to data compiled by American Scientific Enterprise, Inc., several years ago, only 18 percent of corporate new businesses are in the black in two years. On the average, corporate start-ups take seven years to break even, while independent start-ups funded by venture capitalists break even in a little less than four years.

The results of other expectations are derived from myths about new ventures, which must be compared to the realities.

Myth: The most promising young executive or "fast-track" star should be given a chance to show what he or she can do by running a new business.

Reality: The best fast-trackers do not make the best executives for new ventures. Corporate entrepreneurs do, and, as we will show later, these people are decidedly not fast-trackers. Fast-trackers usually remain with a venture only for a couple of years, hardly enough time to learn about the business and certainly not enough time to effect any real changes. Also, they have their sights set on their next promotion.

Myth: The new ventures should operate out of the R&D division because that is where new developments logically fit.

Reality: The new venture should not be in any existing division, even R&D. Not everyone in the corporation will be happy about diversification, or the new venture. Placing the new venture into an existing part of the company may kill it off. The orientation and culture of the R&D organization are antithetical to venturing.

Myth: "Let's give it to Sam. He has enough time to manage the new-venture business. After all, it shouldn't take too much time."

Reality: The new effort will take a lot of management attention in understanding the style of operation, problems specific to corporate venturing, and how to work through those problems with the venturing management.

Myth: The funding has been approved in two phases. That should do it because it allows for contingencies.

Reality: Costs of each venture will not be easily contained. Moreover, most new ventures will have cost overruns. Estimates by entrepreneurs are usually understated by 50 to 60 percent. Few milestones or progress points will be reached on time, adding to costs. Management should not be too optimistic about keeping costs in line, as this can dampen enthusiasm when costs begin to mushroom, and can even cause cancellation of a venture that is really going somewhere. The only way to determine which "cost overruns" are due to poor venture management and which are due to the size of the project legitimately becoming larger is through careful monitoring and handholding with the venture management, which we will discuss later.

IGNORANCE OF THE VENTURING PROCESS

Treating internal new ventures the same as an ongoing business within the company is akin to a death warrant. Many executives are unaware that there is a process for developing new ventures just as there is a process for running the established, ongoing business.

Large corporations must have a defined procedure that permits innovations to surface. And once they are out in the open, there must be a process for selecting and funding the best ideas. Two things must be done in order to successfully find and fund potential businesses:

1. Think of venturing as a distinctive business activity.
2. Develop a professional staff with the skills to find, develop, and nurture ventures.

We will discuss this in a future chapter. The bottom line is that those skills cannot be taught. They must be developed naturally by people who have certain traits to begin with, traits such as analytical skills, interpersonal and negotiating skills, motivation, curiosity, and an ability to understand the "vision" in someone else's idea.

Venture capitalists understand this; very few of them have staffs that handle their evaluations, negotiations, or oversight of ongoing ventures. The principals do their own evaluation of potential ventures. Young venture capitalists may be asked to handle a potential venture from front to back, with coaching from the more experienced members of the operation. With the accumulation of knowledge, an evaluator/investor gets a better sense of whether a potential venture hangs together. Career opportunities in new-business development will encourage people with these special traits to develop them further in a corporate climate rather than going into independent venture capital.

Unless corporations find ways of establishing new-venture evaluation as a career-type assignment, no one will be accumulating the necessary experience to ensure that only the best ideas are selected for development. We will discuss this in detail in Chapter 8.

The Evaluation Process

Screening and evaluation are very complex. The venture must be viewed from every business aspect. Depending on their interests and prior experience, most company reviewers have a single focus in an evaluation; for example, they might concentrate on marketing, technology, or manufacturing. Furthermore, it is usually impossible to find data about a new venture that allows for the kind of evaluation that is possible for an established business or product. The evaluator must understand what is realistic, and work around the limitations to come up with the best answer.

Venture capitalists—the model for success in the development and management of new-business ventures—quickly identify the "deal breakers" in all potential new businesses. As shown previously, they throw out far more ideas in the initial sorting and screening phases than do corporate venture executives. (In the next chapter, we will explain how to find these "deal breakers".)

Political Problems

New businesses compete for management and financial resources with ongoing businesses, and quite naturally lead to political problems within the company. Jealousies are fostered by the perception that special consideration is being given to people in the new venture.

Line management is measured on profit and on its improvement in current business. A new venture may interfere with the achievement of current business objectives by competing for resources and management attention. New-business personnel are concerned that the resources ostensibly committed to new business are vulnerable to priorities associated with the current business. At the same time, line executives fear that the new-business funds may be used up too quickly and that they will be required to fund the venture by diverting resources from current business.

Throughout the product development and in the early stages of commercialization, milestone measurements and periodic reevaluation by the original evaluators greatly increase the likelihood that a new venture will stay on track. This part of the process is almost nonexistent in the corporate environment as part of ad-hoc venturing. As a result, the objectives of the venture become a moving target, and again the chances for survival of a good idea decrease.

TRANSFER PROBLEMS

Transfer refers to the movement of technological innovations from the laboratory to the product-development divisions and to bringing a newly developed business or an acquisition into the corporate structure and merging its operations into the company's ongoing processes.

The problems as they concern new ventures begin with the conflict between the group developing the new venture and the corporation as a whole. Transfer becomes a problem when the new idea is imposed on an existing line organization that is being measured by its contribution to current business.

The number and severity of potential transfer problems require a company to examine the compatibility of the organizations being merged. This necessitates looking at the technologies, types of products and markets, management styles and operations, and the corporate cultures. Many companies have had to contend with substantial problems when bringing a loose, freewheeling, "California" company with a solid ongoing business under the formalistic management policies and procedures of an "eastern" corporation. (Sometimes forcing a merger can discourage the attributes that made the more freewheeling company so attractive in the first place.) These problems are magnified when an unproven startup is involved.

CULTURE CONFLICT

When talking about developing a new venture in the company, executives have the sense that because the organizational structure exists, the effort should be fairly straightforward. They think that some adjustments may be needed, but most problems can be solved with fine tuning. These executives expect the corporate environment to nurture new businesses as well as to pursue ongoing business. The reality of culture conflicts will be discussed in Chapter 6.

Corporate Culture

Corporations are established societies with components characteristic of all cultures: attitudes, procedures, preferences, idols, models, formal interactions, informal operations, and accumulated traditions. Although most executives, and certainly CEOs, know this implicitly, operating executives tend to forget this in the press of everyday activities and particularly when trying to get a new venture going.

This point is well made in a 1980 *Business Week* article:

> Five years ago the chief executives of two major oil companies determined that they would have to diversify out of oil because their current business could not support long-term growth and it faced serious political threats. Not only did they announce their new long-range strategies to employees and the public, but they established elaborate plans to implement them. Today, after several years of floundering in attempts to acquire and build new businesses, both companies are firmly back in oil, and the two CEOs have been replaced.*

Each of the CEOs had been unable to implement his strategy, but not because it was theoretically wrong or bad. One reason they failed appears to be that neither understood that his company's culture was so entrenched in the traditions and values of doing business as "oilmen" that employees resisted—and sabotaged—the radical changes that the CEO tried to impose. Although certain risks are part of the oil business, such as the risk involved in wildcatting and the risks inherent in dealing with foreign governments, the risks in new ventures are different. These risks

---

* "Corporate Culture," *Business Week*, October 22, 1980.

are concerned with the nature of the technology and new products, as well as with radically different markets. This kind of risk is frightening to employees of most companies in well-established, mature industries, such as oil or durable goods.

The CEOs realized too late that diversification strategies can be implemented only with the wholehearted effort and belief of everyone involved. If implementing a diversification strategy violates or conflicts with employees' basic beliefs about the company and their roles, or the traditions that underlie the corporation's culture, the attempts will fail. The same *Business Week* article noted that values in any particular corporate culture, such as aggressiveness, defensiveness, or nimbleness, set a pattern for a company's activities, opinions, and actions.

Management Style

Most top executives lack the perspective necessary for venturing, and end up stifling innovation. This problem was best described by William Abernathy and Robert Hayes of the Harvard Business School in a *New York Times* article when they reported on the sharp increase in the number of CEOs with legal and financial backgrounds.* They described "three bedrock principles" of these managers as "being a skilled strategist," "to oversee the complex processes involved in managing a large organization," and "quickness and decisiveness," which, over the long term, can seriously degrade a company's ability to compete. The current orientation of management does not include devel-

---

* "Management Minus Invention," professors William J. Abernathy and Robert H. Hayes, Harvard Graduate School of Business Administration, *New York Times*, August 20, 1980.

oping "an environment that will nurture new technologies, open up new markets, and develop more productive people." Rather, "a different breed of manager is needed," who knows technologies and markets well enough so that he or she can break the old rules through innovation.

The nature of the entrepreneurial effort in a small business is very different from that in a large corporation. Mental pictures of entrepreneurs are not far removed from stereotyped images of inventors or scientists. Success usually forces them to conform to business standards in dress and behavior. But the entrepreneurial organization itself does not change so readily.

One indicator reflecting the difference in the management style required for an established business versus that of an entrepreneurial start-up is that venture capitalists feel that the entrepreneurial CEO must usually be replaced when the start-up has grown to about $15 million in sales.

New ventures in corporations often take on the trappings of an independent entrepreneurial effort. This is purposely fostered by many companies, which give their venture teams greater freedom and fewer administrative responsibilities than other operating units of the company. The newer the nature of the business, the lower the level of control exercised by management. If the business is very new, especially when the application of the technology is new to the company or even to the industry, then most managements take a laissez-faire approach. One reason is that the executives do not know how to run these new ventures. This encourages the core group of employees on the team to behave more like entrepreneurs than like employees in the mainline business. While all this "freewheeling" is necessary for the new venture, the culture clash with the ongoing operation is inevitable.

Operational Characteristics

To get a better understanding of the nature of the differences in terms of business operations, Figure 1-3 compares the operational characteristics for an established business with those for a start-up entrepreneurial company, the "four people in a garage, loft or basement."

For an ongoing business, the environment is, in the extreme case, similar to an "assembly line" with defined roles. Work proceeds from one person to another via established procedures in a routine that has been established over time. Work patterns and relationships are well

Figure 1-3.   Operational Characteristics

ESTABLISHED VS NEW BUSINESS

CHARACTERISTICS	ESTABLISHED	NEW
ENVIRONMENT	DEFINED ROLES	UNSTRUCTURED
DEGREE OF CERTAINTY	KNOWN BUSINESS	EXTREME UNCERTAINTY
	↓	↓
ORGANIZATION	FORMALIZED	INFORMAL
RESOURCES	SUBSTANTIAL	MINIMAL
STAFF	LARGE, SPECIALISTS	SMALL, GENERALISTS
PLANNING	IN-DEPTH	HIGH POINTS
MEASUREMENT	P & L	MILESTONES
PROCEDURES	COMPREHENSIVE	FEW ESTABLISHED
DECISION PROCESS	STAFFED, DELIBERATE, MULTIPLE APPROVAL LEVELS	FAST, SINGLE OR FEW APPROVAL LEVELS
CONTROLS	EXTENSIVE, TIGHT	FEW

formed. The business is well known, as are the product, competition, and so on. The business is profitable, and resources are supplied to sustain or increase the level of success.

Large specialist staffs in finance, planning, and marketing measure performance and project the future in developing tactical and strategic plans. Elaborate procedures dictate the nature of relationships between departments. Multiple levels of approval and extensive and tight controls are designed to reduce risks to the corporation.

On the other hand, new-business operations are generally unstructured, with several key people providing the technical, management, and marketing expertise. Mutual dependence and daily contributions result in intense interaction and well-informed team members. Each one wears more than one hat and usually understands many aspects of the business. The team is constantly aware that the venture is risky. Team members live with uncertainty, which adds to the excitement and challenge.

In most new ventures decisions are made quickly, but not necessarily by one person acting in the way of the 1980s-style corporate manager. Management overlays are missing, and imposing the traditional management structure and requirements on new businesses can kill them.

In one case, a top chemical company, co-investing with a venture capitalist, sent its chief financial officer to evaluate the financial system used in one of its ventures. The CFO found the system not up to his standards and designed a new one. The new system was perfect for a large corporation, but completely inappropriate for the venture. It took great effort from the venture capitalist to revert the venture's financial system back to an appropriate level.

In the established company environment, the attempt

by management to implant new ventures into the existing environment triggers defense mechanisms analogous to an organ transplant, with the need to suppress the "host's" rejection of a "foreign body."

In his article "A Visit to the New Venture Graveyard,"* Norman Fast summarizes the reactions:

> Successful venturing provokes jealousy, resentment, and attempts by established power centers in the company to undermine it or purge it.
> . . . the venture group represents competition for scarce resources: capital, top management time, personnel. The scarcer these resources are, the more threatening the venture group and the more its relationship with operating divisions comes under pressure.

The operating environment and work force must be prepared for venturing if the automatic-rejection syndrome is to be avoided.

---

* "A Visit to the New Venture Graveyard," Norman Fast, Ph.D., *Research Management*, March 1979, pp. 18–22.

Chapter Two

Process: The Business of Running New Businesses

The fundamental reason for looking at the development of new businesses as a process, or as the "business of running new businesses," is that only an integrated approach can address all the problems discussed in Chapter 1. As obvious as it may sound, management needs to reduce the risks of new business development, and that means understanding how it works and how to do it.

Too often, corporations do "ad-hoc venturing," developing a new business in a vacuum. A committee or task force may be set up to evaluate "ideas" for new businesses that conform to messages from management about what new business it would like the company to go into.

With a preconceived idea of what the new business "should" be, the task force or committee sets out, looks at possible businesses, shapes and hones one until it is ready to be "created" as a business, and recommends it to management. Management then allocates resources for it (usually not enough) and assigns the new business to an operating unit of the company, where it competes with on-going businesses for management time and intangible resources.

The other extreme, which also occurs too often, is that a company has absolutely no idea what business it would like to be in and assigns a committee or task force to look into areas in which the company should develop new businesses.

This task force or committee, working without criteria, often carries a host of ideas through the evaluative stages of new-business creation and sometimes into the actual product-development stage before finding that the business is not feasible, or is not a good match with the company, or presents some other kind of problem that forces the committee to drop the idea.

The primary objectives of a good new-business process are to increase the number of ideas that are generated and submitted and to insure that poor ideas are dropped quickly and that available resources are expended on the good ideas.

WHY THE VENTURE CAPITALIST MODEL?

The major reason for using the venture-capitalist model is that it works. Also, it can be taught and learned by people with appropriate talent, and the fact that it has been used on thousands of ideas and ventures attests to its broad applicability. The process is not complicated by esoteric techniques, nor does it entail convoluted thinking. It is mostly common sense. As with any art, it requires rigor and discipline while concurrently affording flexibility and allowing for creativity.

Evaluating the Proposal

The life of a venture-capital deal is quite simple. Venture capitalists have "deal flows," i.e. they receive a certain rate of proposals. Many entrepreneurs first try to interest a venture capitalist in an idea over the phone. These conversations rarely last longer than 10 minutes, but this is sufficient time for the venture capitalist to get much of the key information that is needed to determine whether to ask for a business plan. In one firm, the secretary is even able to sort the ideas, because the partners have given her a clear idea of the business areas they are interested in for investments.

If a business plan is submitted, the venture capitalist skims it in the first reading to see if the parts "hang together," and makes a few phone calls to people who know a lot about the particular business area.

If the proposal still looks interesting, the venture capitalist usually wants to meet the management team to discuss basic issues such as product, market, management, projections, and financial needs. In these meetings, the venture capitalist tries to find out more about the project and, equally important, to get an impression of the management team.

Venture capitalists then learn as much as possible about the business through written materials about the industry and marketplace, and by speaking with contacts. In this way, venture capitalists develop a body of knowledge about the company, its people, and the market environment in which it has to function.

Venture capitalists vary widely in the degree to which they follow formal procedures. All venture capital groups have a high level of internal communication. Most have weekly meetings at which partners discuss proposals, information obtained, and the evaluation status of proposals.

Some groups do not require any documentation before an investment is made, while others write reports throughout the evaluation process. Corporate venture-capital groups usually require reports—in part to satisfy the corporate control and approval system.

One independent venture-capital partnership holds formal weekly conferences at which all partners briefly discuss each proposal and decide whether it should be moved from the screening into the evaluation phase.

In order to be moved into the evaluation phase, the prospective return on investment should be at least 40–50 percent compounded annually, the market must look promising, and, extremely important, management must be highly rated. Further, there should be at least one apparent way for the venture capitalists to "get out" of the investment—through prospects for the company to go public, a possible merger with another company, or some other alternative.

In the evaluation stage, proposals are evaluated in depth. Management is checked out thoroughly. All partners will meet the management. A thorough business analysis is performed covering areas such as product, market, technology, and finances. If the proposal comes from an operating company, the venture capitalist will visit the plant or laboratory and may, in rare cases, hire consultants to evaluate the work.

The venture capitalist's objective is to identify the critical issues by knowing as much as possible about the market and the people involved. If either management or the venture partnership can come up with viable solutions to any problems that surface and if the partners feel comfortable with the proposal, they will make a conditional decision to finance the venture.

When the deal is structured, the venture capitalists and the management team must be satisfied that any outstanding issues have been resolved. The venture capitalists must feel confident about the management team, and the entrepreneurs must be totally committed to the project.

Working with the Management Team

Assuming the "deal is done," the venture capitalists' level of involvement rises significantly. They will not get involved in day-to-day activities, especially if the venture does well. Rather, the venture capitalists' function is to monitor the venture's progress. At the outset, milestones and schedules are established mutually by both the venture capitalists and the company management. The achievement of these goals serves as a measure of the company's progress.

Frequent communications enable the venture capitalists to stay on top of events. These include representation on the board of directors, visits to the company's facilities, and telephone contacts with members of the management team. Venture capitalists often require monthly reports by functional heads and summaries by the executive officer. Of particular interest are the problems, why they occur and the actions intended to resolve them.

Venture capitalists spend about two days per month on each portfolio company. When things are going well, they have a counseling relationship with the entrepreneur. If problems occur, communications become more frequent and more time is spent with the company. When problems persist and the venture does not do well, the venture capitalists usually take control. In extreme cases, management may be changed.

As the venture-capital fund becomes more fully invested, a larger percentage of each partner's time is spent working with the portfolio companies. Eventually, partners may spend more than half their time in such activities as raising more capital for clients, bank negotiating, and financial planning; they may also get involved in hiring management, supporting strategic planning, handling merger or public-offering negotiations, informally contacting people, and alerting management when they anticipate problems.

After a certain sales level is attained, the venture must take on the characteristics of a mature company. More controls and record keeping are required. In general, the skills and management psychology required are different from those used in starting the venture. The venture capitalists work with the entrepreneurial team to help them through the transition. In many ventures, the management team must be replaced when the venture attains $5 to $15 million in sales. This period produces problems when entrepreneurs realize that they may have to step aside, and at the same time the company may be vulnerable to changes in competition, market, and the product line.

The difficulty of predicting the success of a start-up, even after some time, is demonstrated by the fact that a corporate venture-capital group who had been involved in the first four rounds of financing for Federal Express got out and then returned for the last round. In the intervening time, its share had been diluted, so while the group still made a lot of money, it did not make nearly as much as it would have made had it stayed in the deal the entire time.

THE PROCESS IN SIMPLE FORM

The process used by venture capitalists involves a series of phases that takes a new business from the earliest conceptualization of ideas to commercialization of a product. Although each and every phase must be followed if the process is to yield its best results, it is by no means a mechanistic, checklist process. Rather, it is a dynamic process that allows for the greatest degree of flexibility, while at the same time achieving maximum results in terms of new-business yield.

The process contains four parts: idea generation, transfer, assessment and operation (Figure 2-1).

The first step involves creating a climate for the generation and submission of ideas. We will not deal with this extensively in this book—enough has been written about enhancing creativity—but it is important that for the process to work, employees must be made to understand that *their ideas count.* Even if they don't want to take the time to work through their ideas in the detail required for submission of a business plan—marketing, financial, and commercial analyses—they should be encouraged to submit those ideas and told that they will be part of the "entrepreneurial team" that carries that idea forward if it passes through the process.

The assessment part of the process consists of all of the analyses leading to selection of the idea for development and commercialization—including what is commonly referred to as screening and evaluation—and tracking the idea as it makes its way through the process and becomes a business. The transfer phase occurs after the decision has been made to undertake the venture. Then the operational component begins and continues through development

Figure 2-1.   New Venture Process

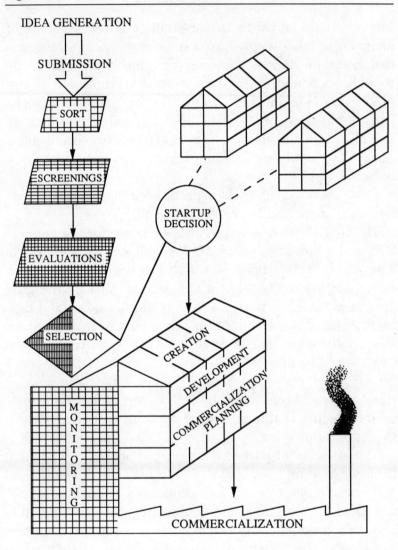

and into commercialization. The monitoring phase, which is part of the assessment component, continues concurrently for the life of the business although the nature of this function will change as the business moves from a development activity to a marketing and sales activity.

The assessment component needs further discussion as the key element in the new-business process. Chapter 3 discusses assessment in a functional context as a series of steps including sorting, screening, evaluation, and sending an idea to development. Assessment is the thread that ties all of the phases of the venture process together. From the time the business plan is submitted and triggers the new-business process, the data base grows. Some type of assessment is performed at all stages in the life of an idea, from its first consideration as a potential business to the time when the product or service is out in the marketplace. The data base built on the core of the business plan provides the continuity between the phases.

Once the ideas are "in the hopper," so to speak, the assessment component of the process begins. This assessment component is made up of five parts:

- Sorting
- Screening
- Evaluating
- Selecting
- Monitoring

After the selection is made, the operational component of the process comes into play. This operational component is made up of four parts:

- Creation
- Development

- Commercialization planning
- Commercialization

Figure 2-2 shows a comparison of the current yield of new businesses for corporations and the yield that can be expected when a new-business process is in place. Notice that while a greater number of ideas are generated and submitted, fewer survive the screening phase when the process is used. The number of ventures that reach the commercial stage is much closer to the number of ventures selected for consideration than when no process is followed.

Four phases of the assessment component are performed before an idea is selected and a venture is established that transforms the idea into a viable business.

The first phase is sorting. The objective is to quickly decide what ideas meet the roughest of criteria. This is done in a binary fashion—yes or no—either it fits the criteria or it doesn't. For example, this one is within an area of competence, this one has no competition and we don't want to break ground, this one fits all of the key criteria—it should be screened. The sorting process should take anywhere from 5 to 15 minutes. The new-business development department meeting could sort 15 to 20 ideas in a morning, provided that the criteria are specific and clear.

The second phase, screening, consists of using major criteria for a general assessment of whether the idea should be evaluated in depth. In almost all companies there is no clear distinction between screening and evaluation. Screening should be done to "see if the pieces hang together," if any major obstacles are immediately evident, and to answer such questions as the likely market acceptance for the product or service, the need for market edu-

Figure 2-2. Results of a New-Business Process

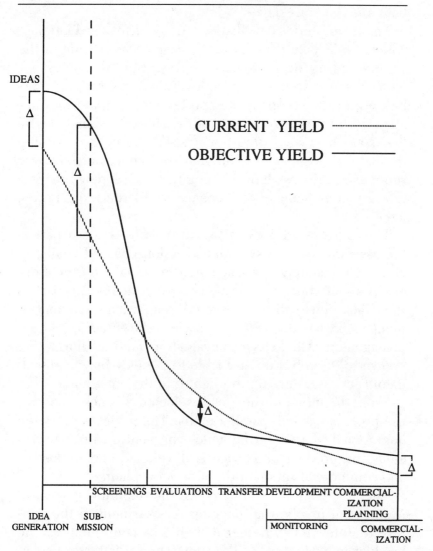

IDEAS

CURRENT YIELD ······························

OBJECTIVE YIELD ————————

SCREENINGS EVALUATIONS TRANSFER DEVELOPMENT COMMERCIAL-
IZATION
PLANNING

IDEA   SUB-
GENERATION   MISSION   MONITORING   COMMERCIAL-
IZATION

cation, and the competitive situation. Screenings should take less than one day.

The third phase is evaluation. An extensive evaluation—which could take from three to six months—leads to the completion of the business case to justify the request for an initial investment. Multiple evaluations may be performed, or the company may prefer one continuous evaluation with interim reports. Additional evaluations may be necessary to answer questions raised during a preceding evaluation. Also, new data may become available over time, especially as all of the members of the new-business development team have a chance to let the idea "percolate."

The fourth, and final, phase in the pre-creation part of the assessment process is the selection phase. Usually, in an ongoing company, management will make the final decision about starting a new business. A detailed report of the evaluations will be presented as a package to management, along with recommendations for funding. Often management will do its own evaluation, adding information known to them but not available to the new-business evaluators and therefore not brought into the equation.

From the moment the idea is selected as a new venture, the process has two parallel paths. The project enters the operational phase, during which the venture team is created, the product or service is developed and packaged, and commercialization of the product is planned.

The assessment continues as the monitoring phase. Monitoring involves an ongoing reassessment of the venture to determine whether it should be continued. As the product moves closer to the time when it is ready for announcement and market release, more and better data becomes available, adding to and improving the information that has been collected. Monitoring, or oversight, as venture capitalists refer to it, is needed to track the project against the plan and is the basis for deciding whether the company still wants to get into the business.

While a good number of companies appear to follow some type of process in general terms, it is at this point, where the process splits in two and the operational part enters the scheme, that any semblance of a process disappears and things tend to break down.

In most instances, the ad-hoc task force or committee that has been set up to evaluate the idea is disbanded at this point, unless it has other new-business ideas it is pursuing. If the company creates the new business that has been recommended, it is usually a decision made by management, and the new business is then transferred into one of the operating units, or else a new operating unit is set up and managers are brought in from other parts of the corporation to run it. In corporate America, very rarely is the "entrepreneur," the individual who had the original idea, allowed to run his or her own business. This person must become a part of the management team.

A key reason failure occurs after the business is set up is that the monitoring phase is either dropped or subsumed by regular corporate reporting and oversight. With the disbanding of the evaluative group, the corporation *often loses sight of the new business's purpose*, and it becomes hard to monitor how well the new business is fulfilling its purpose. If the preselection data base has been destroyed or filed in the archives, it is hard to monitor the new business successfully.

As was said in Chapter 1, a new business is systemically different from an ongoing business, and it must be "nurtured" rather than merely managed.

Venture capitalists have a way of nurturing new businesses—"handholding"—and it entails as much parenting as it does managing.

ADVANTAGES OF THIS NEW-BUSINESS SYSTEM

The goal of a process for venturing is to save the company time, effort, and money over the ad-hoc approach. The new-business process, when correctly implemented, provides three distinct advantages over ad-hoc venturing:

- Continuity
- Comprehensiveness
- Consistency

Continuity

There must be a flow, a smooth movement from one phase of the process to the next. A new-business team cannot suddenly decide to go through an in-depth evaluation of the first idea that pops up. If an idea does not meet the criteria at any given stage of the process, and is still evaluated in depth, there had better be a compelling reason not to discard it.

There must be linkage between phases. The output from one phase should be the major input into the next phase. Questions and concerns not answered in the previous phase must be addressed here. At each step of the process, the assessment stream must answer the major question, Is this worth doing? or, Is this worth continuing?

The data base created by the people who conduct evaluations of possible ventures should not be destroyed, either physically thrown away or filed with all of the working papers of the group. Instead, it must be retained for use during monitoring and for the next evaluation. Otherwise, in an ad-hoc approach, the next group that comes along to do an evaluation will not have the benefit of this group's experience.

Comprehensiveness

The process must include all aspects of getting into the new business. It must provide for continued testing as to whether the proposed venture should be undertaken. The assessment component of new-business development cannot end when the evaluation phase is over. Those who have worked through all the assessment phases of a new venture are in the best position to make a final decision about selecting whether to go ahead with the development.

Those same people are also the most qualified to continue monitoring and nurturing the new business, by virtue of the fact that if management decides to go with it, they have internalized the vision of the new company and of the entrepreneur who had the idea. While outsiders might be able to objectively monitor the company, insiders have a commitment to the process and will nurture the company, providing the proper amount of oversight balanced with the handholding necessary for a comprehensive approach.

Consistency

Screening and evaluation is an art. One has to be in the business of evaluating, developing, and nurturing new businesses for a while to be able to practice and refine the art.

It is impossible to be consistent if different people are

undertaking each evaluation, or if the people who are monitoring development efforts are different from those who evaluated the development plan and decided that the business should be started. The only way to ensure that the new-business development process is performed the same way every time is to have an organization responsible for new-business development, whose sole purpose is to find new business ideas, create new businesses, and monitor those businesses.

Consistency can be achieved only through the clear definition of new-business objectives and the creation of a new-business strategy that includes a new-business development group of some kind, a permanent—if not always active—group of individuals who evaluate new-venture opportunities.

Chapter Three

Assessing the Proposed Venture

The largest and most difficult piece of the new-venture business puzzle is the screening and evaluation process. This assessment part consists of five phases. Throughout all five phases, the objective is to "find the fatal flaw," the "deal breaker" that will kill a venture somewhere down the line. The goal is to eliminate fatally flawed ideas as early as possible, thereby saving precious time and money further down the new-venture process. A collateral objective is to develop a plan to overcome potentially serious but not fatal problems.

At the outset, it is important to realize that evaluation is an art, not a science. In this chapter we will not describe any specific techniques, but rather the thought process that can make assessment more effective with a minimum of time and effort. There is no one scheme that always works for picking winning ventures, and it is certainly not mechanistic.

Corporate analyses tend to take too long and waste money, and analysts may fail to validate the data presented. Assessment, when done properly, combines both analysis and intuition, and requires the ability to trust one's own "gut" reactions and to live with the decisions that follow. The ability and the courage to make these decisions—and the willingness to live with them—increases with experience, and in direct proportion to the executive management's acceptance of these decisions. Only a person who has done assessments over and over again, and put together a knowledge base to complement a natural aptitude, can be successful. But that person also needs management's backing.

The first three phases of the assessment cycle—sorting, screening, and evaluation—lead to the decision to invest in a venture.

Sorting provides the filter through which ideas are given a simple yes or no based on a few straightforward criteria, such as whether the idea fits a company's chosen business area, investment level, feasibility, market, and technology, as they apply to the ventures the company wants to start.

Screening begins to examine the venture ideas that have passed the initial sort. The screening applies more subjective standards, such as the quality of management, the market, the product and its relation to current products (both in the company's repertoire and outside it), the state of technology, and ballpark financial projections.

In the evaluation phase, each of these areas is developed more closely to see if it will stand up to the scrutiny of an in-depth analysis necessary to make the decision to launch the venture. A number of questions must be asked about each of the subjective criteria, including:

- Is the management team compatible?
- How much experience does it have?
- How much entrepreneurial experience?

- What are the market channels?
- What is the competition?
- Who are the potential customers?
- Does the product have proprietary advantages?
- What is its relationship to the rest of the company's product line?
- How can it be configured to work with other products?
- Is the technology available and feasible, or does it require a breakthrough?
- What is the expected return on investment, price, profit margin, cost, and payback period?
- Are there potential regulatory problems, legal issues, union and worker relations problems?

These factors must be constantly reevaluated during the monitoring of ventures that are actually developed.

TRICKS OF THE TRADE

There are two basic rules for screening and evaluating possible new ventures:

1. Look at the potential new venture as a business system.
2. At each step of the assessment process, simulate the viability of the enterprise.

By having these two guidelines throughout the assessment cycle, doing a complete evaluation will be something like making a decision tree. Throughout the screening and evaluation, the question should be asked: if we go in this direction, what are all the possible things that could go wrong? The question is always, How can things go wrong? not, How can things go right?

Too often, when corporations are looking to start new businesses, a new-venture task force comes up with the ideas themselves, then analyzes those ideas, massaging the numbers until they have come up with the perfect scenario, under which the business will run perfectly. This is less likely to happen when ideas come to a new-venture business from outside—from "entrepreneurs" within the company—but it still occurs.

Because of this tendency, there are two guidelines for screening and evaluating new-venture candidates.

Validate the Data

First of all, validate the data that is given. See how it hangs together, intuitively at first, then by the numbers. As a potential venture passes each step in the screening and evaluating process, the "entrepreneur" should be asked to provide more details. (This will be discussed more completely in the chapters on the business plan and the venture-business charter.) While the venture-business principals may point the entrepreneur in the right direction about where to find information and how to develop data, the entrepreneur should be the one to come up with the figures. Then the venture-business principals can test the information.

People have a tendency to believe anything that is in print, and to assume that it is correct, truthful, and accurate. Information coming from the entrepreneur or product champion is considered virtually unquestionable. After all, who knows more than the person working on the idea? At a recent course on evaluating new ventures, a participant said, "I never knew there was anything to validate because all the information I needed was in the proposal."

Data validation must begin with the business plan and continue as more information becomes available. In validating, evaluators will always be looking for consistency as a first step, continually using their intuition. Ultimately, they will "run numbers." The consistency check, which involves checking data against other information in the business plan, then with other sources of information, requires that the reader understand and pay attention to the information provided. Very often the flaws can be derived from the proposal itself.

Intuition about data can help in screening and evaluating more than many people realize. Some data just doesn't hold up to the basic and simple questions, such as, Does it make sense? and, Is it based on realistic assumptions? For instance, in 1985 it was found that a young medical researcher had written literally dozens of academic papers published in top medical journals, based on fraudulent data. Although many of the papers had been "coauthored" by senior researchers, who ostensibly had checked the data, then refereed by peers before appearing in the journals, everyone had overlooked such data as a family tree where a 13-year-old boy had several children. Once the researcher's fraud had been discovered and people again rechecked his research, this bit of data jumped right off the page, but no one had bothered to check it before.

Screen Every Project Twice

The second guideline requires that every project be screened at least twice to reduce bias and increase the probability of a correct recommendation. These two screenings should be done by two different people, one of whom should be the venture-business principal who is working with the entrepreneur to develop the proposal.

Laws of Data Analysis

Along with these two rules about how to deal with the proposal and with the data itself, there are two fundamental laws of data analysis that should be kept in mind when screening and evaluating venture candidates.

1. *The quality and quantity of data are worse the further away the market reality is.* If a venture is dealing with a state-of-the-art product that is extending a market (even if the company considering the venture is not in that market), the data needed to project that venture's success may be available from existing information. But if the venture will need breakthrough technology, and there is no market that exists for that technology, some data about that venture would be impossible to develop.

Too many people look for data that does not exist, or they try to do things with the data that just can not be done at the time the analysis is being conducted. This is especially true in larger companies, where executive management often instinctively rejects any presentation that is based on "incomplete" analysis.

2. *Not all criteria are equally applicable to all ventures at all phases of the venture's development.* Not all criteria need to be used in evaluating every venture.

Figure 3-1 shows some of the different criteria that should be considered at each stage of the venture assessment and the approximate weight (the width of the bands and the crosshatching) of those categories of criteria at each

Figure 3-1. Assessing New Business Opportunities

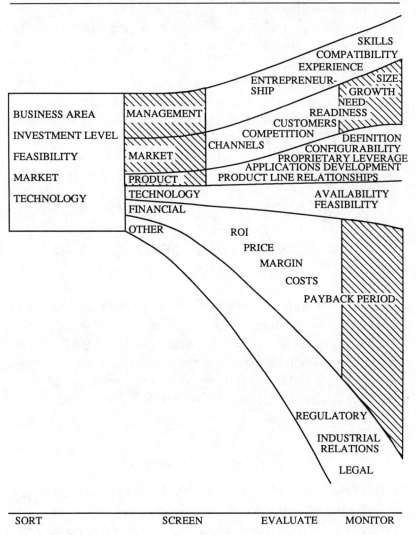

SORT   SCREEN   EVALUATE   MONITOR

stage. Note that the areas that are stressed in the evaluation phase—the detailed phase of looking at a venture—
are also followed closely when the venture is monitored
throughout its life. We will return to this diagram throughout this chapter.

A final rule on successful evaluation is that the same person should perform all of the steps. This is not to say that
one person must have all the skills. Specialists should be
used to provide unique skills. But one person should have
the responsibility for understanding the entire venture
well enough to make decisions based on both evidence and
intuition.

COMMON PITFALLS IN SCREENING AND EVALUATION

There are a number of problems that crop up time and
time again in the screening and evaluation of venture candidates, especially in a corporate environment. While
some are human nature, the corporate environment puts
pressure on those who analyze businesses to behave in
ways that are anathema to successful venture development.

Unrealistic Standards

One of the greatest problems is that corporations have high
standards for what a good business analysis—screening and
evaluation—looks like, based on their experience with
their mainline business. Many businesses think there is, in
effect, a textbook formula for screening and evaluating new
businesses.

They want to see return on investment (ROI) analyses.

They want to see multiple projections covering a wide range of scenarios and contingencies. They want to see a lot of data included in the analysis, believing it will reduce the risk. As a result, an analysis may include information that is unproductive and inconsequential. They want to see the numbers run and run and run.

This leads to the condition of *analysis paralysis.*

Analysis paralysis is not easy to cure, especially not in a corporate environment. As has been mentioned before, the typical model for venture analysis within corporations is to form one-time committees or task forces periodically to develop new businesses. These committees often have mandates to look in certain areas, to find the best potential businesses. The members individually, and certainly collectively, are most often feeling their way around in the world of new-business development. They want to make sure to cover all the bases.

Committees within corporations usually make a number of mistakes. They fail to determine what is truly important out of all the data explored. More often than not, they apply criteria inappropriately and treat everything equally, thereby coming out with skewed results. Because these committees are so often made up of people from the three primary areas of the company—the financial, the marketing, and the purely technical—more often than not this means too heavy an emphasis on the financial picture early on, too closely analyzing a market before it is clear that a market exists, and overplaying the technology—not realizing how difficult it may be to make the technology feasible. The major weakness in these analyses is the lack of focus on management—finding the right kind of team to run the new business. The assumption is that it will be staffed by managers who have done well in other areas of the business.

Overemphasis on Numbers

Another problem takes the form of an overemphasis on quantitative analysis, which is based on the assumption that if there are more numbers the analysis is inherently more accurate. What develops is a false sense of accuracy, and worse, a false sense of security. ROIs are generated too early in the process, and end up being worthless.

Inability to Simulate Product Viability

Corporate analysts have great difficulty simulating the entire business process, from setting up an office to getting the product out the door and having customers like it. The analysts who make up the committee or task force are individuals, each having a particular area of interest. They may have trouble seeing other parts of the analysis, and the putting together of the final presentation becomes a political battle. There needs to be one person who has a sense of all the diverse elements involved and who can integrate them into a coherent analysis.

Focus on Easy Things First

People have a tendency to do the easy things first. As a result, tying together key items may not get done.

Corporate Mentality

The overriding culture of corporations, as well as the hierarchy inherent in most corporations, also comes into play in the inability to generate successful new businesses. The corporate dictum is: don't look dumb! But the venture dictum is: make decisions, even if you look dumb! Because the more decisions you make, the more you analyze those decisions after the fact and find out *why* the dumb ones were dumb, the greater the chances are next time of not making a dumb decision.

Sterilizing the Presentation

Another problem of business analysis within corporations is that by the time the committee or task force makes its presentation to executive management it is no longer necessarily the committee's presentation, but the presentation of all the managers in the middle who believe—and often rightly so in the corporate environment—that the suggestions made by a committee reflect on them as managers, as the people who have oversight of the area in which the committee is working.

The committee takes its presentation to a first-line manager, who says, "The pitch needs to be changed, and it's missing this element." The element is added and the pitch changed. It is then taken to the second-line manager, who says, "It needs to be framed this way for the management committee." So it is reframed. By the time it reaches those who rule on it, it is no longer a presentation by the committee on a new type of business—it has become the kind of presentation that the management committee is used to hearing, a presentation that relies on the old ways of doing business.

SIMULATING VIABILITY—WILL THIS DOG HUNT?

Assessing viability begins with looking at the business as an integrated whole. To do this, an analyst must examine the business plan as if the business were ongoing. This requires looking at the three I's of Integration.

Interfaces: relationships between the prospective business and vendors, suppliers, distributors, shippers, and wholesalers, as well as other parts of the corporation.

Interactions: activities that go on between the organizations involved in the interfaces; such as purchases of materials and parts, product distribution, service arrangements, and administration.

Interdependencies: sole-source suppliers, exclusive marketing arrangements, imported parts, unique customer values, and industrial relations.

A business must be thought of in terms of its ultimate objective. The purpose of the business is to take the idea for a product or service, obtain the "parts" and "materials" necessary, and produce the product or service, then sell it. A proposed venture must be thought of in the same way, as a flow from idea to end-product in the market.

The key question is whether it can happen. Is it feasible to carry this idea from the information given by the entrepreneur on paper to a flesh-and-blood business, with people producing a product or service and successfully selling it in the marketplace?

Although this may seem obvious, it is contrary to the way businesses are usually evaluated. Business analysts rarely think of businesses as an integrated whole. Business analyses are generally undertaken in a piecemeal fashion, and if several aspects are analyzed at the same time, the pieces will be brought together in a report. Most often one person will examine the finances, another person the market, another person the technology, and another the legal, regulatory, and industrial-relations issues. These facets of the business are analyzed individually rather than as a whole, interdependent system; they are examined in terms of what will happen at a given point in time rather than as a metamorphosis from an idea into a business, with the associated dynamics. Being able to assess viability demands that one person be responsible for integrating the total analysis.

THE STAGES IN DETAIL

Sorting

Sorting requires finding simple answers to a few basic questions; such as does this idea meet this particular criteria? The final decision as to whether a potential venture should be pursued to the screening phase can and should be made in a very short period of time—anywhere from 5 to 15 minutes. If the criteria for making the sort decision are crystal clear, the decision can be made in a minute.

Companies rarely make an explicit decision to look at a particular new idea in detail. They jump into evaluating the idea in depth without having decided whether the idea meets the most basic criteria. There are often no explicit criteria reflecting management's interests. Guidelines to establish the boundaries for new ventures are sometimes developed after the company knows the types of businesses being proposed. Often, the same criteria are not applied consistently to all ideas. Too often managers say, "It seems worth exploring," or "There's no harm in taking a look at it."

But there is harm—wasted resources, ambivalence, diluting efforts on worthwhile activities, disappointment, and often management's ultimate disaffection with venturing.

New-Venture Strategy

The starting point of the sort is a new-venture strategy. All companies are familiar with and develop strategies. However, very few look at new-business opportunities as a distinct activity. Instead, most plans provide for continuation of the current business with a new product included to the degree that resources can be spared and funds afforded.

Top management must develop a new-business plan that allocates resources separately from the current business.

The strategy should come out of a "gap analysis," an analysis of where the company is today, where it wants to be tomorrow, and how it might bridge the gap. It entails an assessment of the company's skills, principal resources, current business profile, and its cultural climate. Management needs to look at growth areas, selecting areas where the company would be able to use core skills to enter into a new market or industry. Within these areas, the company should identify market niches and the capabilities required for entry and participation.

IBM's entry into the biomedical business traded on the company's core skills in signal processing, data transmission, signal analysis, pattern recognition, and precision measurement by computer to create a computerized electrocardiogram system that obviated human error and enabled doctors to concentrate on the EKGs identified as abnormal.

Grumman used its metal-forming skills to get into the bus business. It was producing aircraft, which means it was already in the transportation business, and had knowledge of small- and large-scale movement of people and transportation systems.

A well-known producer of fine jewelry took its capability for quality and precision watches into timing mechanisms for industrial equipment. The company also capitalized on its tooling and metals research for its watches and luxury items to go into custom-development of metals for unique applications.

A company's strategy becomes the framework for the new-venture program. The identified niches are explored and discussed with people throughout the corporation. Proposals are solicited in the identified areas. This plan enables the company to determine the key criteria and major policy considerations for selecting prospective ventures.

From a good new-venture strategy will come enough information to establish sorting criteria.

Sorting Criteria

Drawing on the experience of venture capitalists, there appear to be five primary criteria for selecting or rejecting new-venture proposals. Each company must define these criteria for themselves:

- **Business area:** business areas of interest
- **Investment level:** initial funding and total investment required (usually given as a range)
- **Feasibility:** state-of-the-art, development, or research ventures
- **Market:** type
- **Technology:** technologies the company sees as having significant product potential in the future

Any new-venture business—either within a corporation or an independent fund—must set limits in these five areas for sorting proposals. It must also decide how many of these parameters must be met and which of the parameters should be weighted more heavily than others. With these ground rules, the new-venture business staff will have latitude in bringing proposals forward. Figures 3-2 and 3-3 show the sorting criteria for a number of independent and corporate venture-capital groups.

The list of sorting criteria may include other major considerations. Companies may want to limit new ventures to those that will utilize existing sales and distribution channels, where the technology is related to company capability, or to those that will reflect a desirable image.

Some factors have questionable value in sorting. Proprietary leverage can be determined only after considerable analysis of the product and the market. Uniqueness of product and patent protection is controversial as a sorting criterion. Venture capitalists and companies disagree on its value. Some prefer business areas where there is competition, which suggests that there is a market, thereby reducing the risk. Other companies believe the cost of developing the market is less than entering an established market and trying to obtain a meaningful market share.

As with any set of rules, there will be exceptions. The list should not supersede judgment, but should represent management's thinking before it has looked at any proposals.

The list is really a list of "comfort factors." Sorting combines these comfort factors and creates a "comfort index" that can be used to rank prospective ventures. Investors need to be comfortable with their investments, and in that respect, a new venture is no different from any other type of investment.

Figure 3-2.   Sorting Criteria,
Independent Venture Capital Partnerships

VENTURE CAPITAL "A"	VENTURE CAPITAL "B"
PREFERRED BUSINESS AREAS	
Home Entertainment	"Manufacturing-based
Communications	companies in technology or
Computers & Related Products	growth industrial or consumer
High Technology	markets"
Medium Technology	
AREAS AVOIDED	
CATV	Chemicals & Plastics
Construction	Construction
Food (Processing,	Food (Franchising)
Franchising)	Hotels, Motels, Restaurants
Hotels, Motels, Restaurants	Real Estate
Leasing	
Metals	
Motion Pictures	
Natural Resources	
Real Estate	
Retailing & Wholesaling	
INITIAL INVESTMENT	
350,000 - 750,000	100,000 - 1.5 Million
TOTAL INVESTMENT	
AVERAGE/MAXIMUM	
400,000/800,000	500,000 - 700,000/2.5 Million
MATURITY OF COMPANY DESIRED	
Startups	Seed Financings
Second, Third Round Financings	Startups
Bridge Financings	Second, Third Round Financings
Buyouts	Bridge Financings
	Buyouts
PREFERRED LOCATION	
West Coast	

Too often companies take the "it's-worth-a-try" approach, with the result that they lose almost 100 percent of the time. There are enough uncertainties to be dealt with in venturing; corporations need to control as many variables as possible.

Assuming that the new-venture business will be ongoing, and not a one-time attempt to find a new business, each potential new business must be considered within the

Figure 3-3. Sorting Criteria,
Corporate Venture Capital Groups

BANK	OFFICE EQUIPMENT COMPANY	OIL COMPANY
PREFERRED BUSINESS AREAS		
CATV	CATV	Computer Hardware
Chemicals & Plastics	Communications	Electronic Data Processing
Computer Hardware & Software	Computer Software	Electronic & Electric
Consumer Products	Electronic Data Processing	Components
Electronic Data Processing	Electronic & Electric Components	Optics & Lasers
Electronic & Electric Components	High Technology	Proprietary Technology
Environmental Control	Proprietary Technology	High Technology
Food (Processing & Franchising)	Optics & Lasers	
General, No Preference		
Health Services		
High Technology		
Leisure Time		
Manufacturing		
Marketing		
Medical Equipmt. & Instrumentation		
Medium Technology		
Metal Fabrication & Processing		
Metallurgy		
Non-Technical		
Optics & Lasers		
Pharmaceuticals		
Proprietary Technology		
Retailing & Wholesaling		
Service		
AREAS AVOIDED		
Construction	Chemicals & Plastics	Consumer Products
Education	Food (Franchising)	Construction
Finance & Financial Services	Hotels, Motels, Restaurants	Food (Franchising)
Hotels, Motels, Restaurants	Pharmaceuticals	Hotels, Motels, Restaurants
Leasing	Real Estate	Leasing
Motion Pictures		Leisure Time
Natural Resources		Medium Technology
Real Estate		Motion Pictures
Oil & Gas		Non-Technical
		Real Estate
		Retailing & Wholesaling
		Service
INITIAL INVESTMENT		
300,000 - 5 Million	100,000 - Open	500,000 - Open
TOTAL INVESTMENT AVERAGE/MAX		
1M/5 Million	Open/Open	Open/Open
MATURITY		
Startups	Seed Financings	Buyouts
Second, Third Round Financings	Startups	
Bridge Financings	Second, Third Round Financings	
Buyouts	Bridge Financings	
	Buyouts	
PREFERRED LOCATION		
Continental U.S.		

context of other new businesses being developed or considered. Portfolio analysis is as critical in venturing as in any other type of prudent investing.

If the pool of money given to the new-venture business is $20 million, it could have the stipulation that no more than $3 million will be spent on any one start-up and that there should be a technological balance. If there are already two ventures that require advancing the state of the art or obtaining a breakthrough in technology, the next venture should probably be one that uses state-of-the-art technology.

Screening

The second stage of the assessment cycle is screening. Screening begins the serious investigation of a prospective new business. The criteria are broader, and require subjective judgment. In the screening phase, the evaluator must begin simulating the viability of the venture. This is to show how all pieces fit and could work together. The evaluator must look for the three I's of integration: interfaces, interactions, and interdependencies. Most of the analysis is qualitative, even though some aspects can be quantified.

Venture capitalists and companies usually use the same criteria to evaluate a business opportunity. Venture capitalists consider management, market, and product the three most important criteria at this point. The other three criteria, which will come to play a more important role later, are technology, finances, and "other factors."

Management

Venture capitalists consider the management team the most crucial element in starting a new venture. They recognize that rarely is there one individual who has all the key talents of a management team. As a result they ask the entrepreneur to come in with a suggested team. They consider this so important that if a team is not available, they will search for appropriate personnel if the project and the entrepreneur are otherwise attractive to them.

A recent study supports the venture-capitalist approach, albeit for different reasons. The study found that partnerships are more likely to be successful than sole proprietorships, for two reasons. Sole owners tend to lose their sense of direction, while in a partnership at least one partner will usually be focused on the objective. Additionally, the mutual support one gives the other will keep interest high.

Key factors when looking for members of a management team are their individual expertise, experience and track record, commitment, entrepreneurial spirit, and whether they have worked together before.

Corporations usually think in terms of an individual to run the venture. They may choose the entrepreneur or the product champion or they may "plug in" a competent manager from another part of the business. Rarely do they evaluate the entrepreneurial qualities of the individual who is supposed to make a success of the venture. And even more rarely do they think of a team with complementary skills and emotional balance.

Even when the entrepreneur or product champion is chosen to head the venture, other senior managers are usually chosen on the basis of traditional, big-company management criteria. This corporate model of staffing senior management of new businesses with "good managers" from other, ongoing parts of the company is a major factor contributing to the lack of success of companies in starting new businesses. Often the person selected is due for promotion, or has "been around long enough." Companies also use the situation as a training ground for "fast-track" employees. They reason that even if it does not work out, at least the general manager will learn something and be better prepared for the next promotion.

The lack of a coherent management team also plays into the hands of fickle executives, who often appoint a new chief executive to head the venture every two or three years. In one such situation "Jim" was responsible for a product when it was classed and sold as a research machine. When a new venture was built on the strength of the product's fulfilling a critical need, he was brought in to head up the marketing function. He had an entrepreneurial orientation, was committed to the venture and its products, and had learned the nuances of the business. In most of the detailed day-to-day operations, Jim worked with his counterparts in the other functions to keep the business going when he was not bringing a new general manager up to speed.

When the company decided to abort the venture after years of substantial losses, Jim raised capital and wanted to buy the business. Instead, the company sold off the product lines to different companies and never considered its in-house entrepreneurial potential.

The message is clear: companies must be willing to look for individuals with the skills and the entrepreneurial commitment to lead the new business successfully. They must look for the entrepreneurial talent within the company and resist the temptation to bring in a good "manager." Even going outside for an entrepreneurial manager could injure the company's internal venturing effort.

The company must ask, Has the management team—the group picked to be the venture's executives—ever worked together? If not, do they appear to be compatible? Is there a proper balance of skills within the management team? And what is the track record of these people, both as a team and as individuals? Most important, what are their entrepreneurial accomplishments, rather than their accomplishments as corporate managers?

Market

Although the screening phase begins with a given set of assumptions, these are not set in stone for the duration of the assessment cycle. In any given week a number of the variables being explored could change. No screening will come up with decisions that can be taken to the bank. Rather, screening provides a snapshot that can be blown up, one sector at a time, and evaluated further and in far greater detail.

Many analysts accept the market as identified by the entrepreneur, then put limits on the market, types of prospects, buying power, demographic characteristics, and other variables. Although this is necessary for complete evaluation of the market, it should be done only after defining what the customers want and how badly they want it.

Too often inventors and corporations decide to give the customers what they "need" rather than what they want. This presumptive thinking has spelled trouble for many people and companies over the years. It may be okay to give customers what they need, but only if it is packaged as something they want. A former director of marketing for Radio Shack had it right when he titled his book *To Catch a Mouse, Make a Noise Like a Cheese.*

There are three guidelines for establishing need:

1. **Validate the requirement**—Does the need exist? Identify the basic problem or desire that the product or service is supposed to address. Who wants it solved? How exactly will the solution deal with the problem? When and under what circumstances will they use the solution?

2. **Justify the requirement**—How important is it that the need be met? How widespread is the problem and the prospective market for the particular solution? Within that is an assessment of priorities for a solution. The problem may be more urgent for some than for others, and the obvious user may not be part of the proposed market.

3. **Quantify the market**—Is there value to meeting the need? What price is the proposed customer willing to pay for the solution? Are there enough people willing to pay that price to make producing the solution worthwhile?

Characteristics of the market—such as whether it is price-sensitive, attracted by technology, stable, fad-oriented, and has a long purchase-decision cycle—and after-market opportunity, determine the quality of the market and market potential.

Sometimes a product seems too good to let go, even if it means searching for a market. The story is often told about the electric knife. Developed in response to the presumed need for ease in slicing roasts, fowl, and other meats, initial sales were poor. A new executive for the company suggested that the product be marketed as a gift item. In this context, the advertising focused on the gift giver's need to find something that people would not normally buy for themselves. Because it was useful in the kitchen and classed as a nonessential, most gift givers could be fairly sure that it was a viable gift. Sales were very good that first Christmas. Of course, a lot of electric knives have been sitting in closets for years. The size of an initial market does not make for lasting success, and forcing an item into a niche is not always wise.

Product

A number of questions must be asked about the product. What exactly is the product? Is the technology to make the product available? If not, what will need to be done to make it available? Is the product within the state of the art for what it is supposed to do, or are other technological breakthroughs needed to make the product useful? What is this product's relationship to the rest of the company's product line, and what impact will it have on the other products in the product line?

Does the product have any proprietary leverage—is it patented or patentable? Does it have a trademark or other form of legal protection? How long will this advantage hold up, both legally and in terms of development and bringing to market of similar products that do not infringe on the product's proprietary nature?

Other Screening Considerations

Detailed forecasting to arrive at market demand, sales projections for the first five years after product release, income-to-expense ratios, and return-on-investment should not be done at this time. This requires a level of detail that is inconsistent with the objective of the screening phase. Moreover, studies have shown that the greater the degree of product newness the less accurate the forecast. The maximum effort that is recommended here is a ballpark estimate.

The only financial considerations that must be taken into

account at this point are very rough estimates of the magnitude of costs, projected pricing, and payback period.

The business plan itself must be questioned closely in each iteration of its preparation. The first screening may be based on a very preliminary business plan. The plan must be realistic and describe a business that is compatible with the company's new-business strategy.

There are also a host of "factor X" considerations that may pop up in the development of a new business, and these should be considered as early as possible. Among them are

- Legal and regulatory issues
- Health and safety issues
- Internal corporate environment issues
- Industrial relations issues

Evaluation

In the evaluation phase, the major areas explored in the screening stage must be broken up into finer points, and the evaluation must be more complete. Among the issues that must be delved into in great depth are

Financial:

- financial characteristics of the business
- pricing and profit margin
- forecasts and growth potential

Marketing:

- market entry and marketing strategy
- market characteristics and trends

- competitive environment
- distribution channels

Product and Technology:

- manufacturing issues

Management Skills and Capabilities:

- All of these are sufficiently broad and deep to preclude discussion here. Trying to describe when and how each should be used could only be done in the context of a number of case studies. Here, we can only describe some of the more overriding considerations that evaluators should be concerned with.

The Corporate Environment and Culture

Culture, a key ingredient in the overall success of venturing, is equally important in considering the market, type of product, distribution channels, and style of operations associated with any new business.

Certainly, situations must be taken into account where management would feel uncomfortable dealing with certain market segments, is concerned about image impact, and is unfamiliar with the terms and conditions of doing business with new groups of suppliers, vendors, and distributors. These situations are not show stoppers, but require attention and will affect costs, progress, and success.

Proprietary Position

One would assume that any investor would jump at an opportunity where the company had a patent or proprietary position. However, few people would want a patent position so exclusive that nobody wants to buy it. Conservative venture capitalists indicate that they would have more patience and wait longer for a proprietary product. Most companies and corporate venture capitalists stress that a proprietary position or uniqueness of the product is essential.

Market Factors

Venture capitalists look at the market opportunities, the channels, the potential for international sales, and the pricing structure. They are concerned with issues such as accessibility to the market, fast or at least good market growth, the product's ability to fill a void in the marketplace, the market's readiness for the product, and the market's being immediate and in place. For venture capitalists investing in high-technology products, the market must welcome innovation.

Companies usually go into a lot more detail in this analysis than venture capitalists do. For example, 3M tries to find as many applications as possible and identify as many customer groups as possible at the outset. As 3M has successfully demonstrated, it is oriented toward minor market niches where it has established near-monopolies in the areas it enters.

A large industrial organization in the automotive aftermarket, as well as OEM market for capital equipment, wants its market analyses to identify market niches and many small businesses to establish footholds in a diverse range of markets.

In all cases investors, product managers, and analysts are concerned with how a market will be penetrated and the contingency plans available if the initial penetration is not successful.

Industry and Competition

Although some of these points are implicit in the evaluation of the market, venture capitalists' thoughts reflect some nuances in competitive evaluation. They look for justification for a competitive venture in terms of products, processes, and the emergence of future competition. While most of them look for the proprietary edge over the competition, some, like Bill Draper, formerly the head of Sutter Hill Ventures, specifically ask, "Is the competition healthy?" If so, it indicates a healthy, growing market.

A more conservative venture capitalist looks for niches in the market that are not so large as to attract competition. People in one corporate venture-capital department question whether the dynamics of the industry are such that the venture's operations would be compatible and function well. One analytically oriented independent venture capitalist looks for the potential for the venture to become a significant factor in a particular market. His objective is to find "a market where everybody gets rich. There, you can mess up a lot and the company can still survive."

LIFE CYCLES

Investors, analysts, and companies think of products in terms of life cycles. At its outset a product is bought by the leading edge of the market, the "innovators," followed by the "early adopters," and then by greater numbers of the "early majority," until peak sales are reached. Then sales decline and at the later stages the product is bought by the "laggards." (This schema was developed by Everett M. Rogers with F. Floyd Shoemaker in the book *Communication of Innovations.* *)

New versions of products have complete life cycles of their own, and theoretically, as product modifications become more advanced technologically, the market should expand. This does not always happen. It may happen that they become a point on the life cycle of a *type* of product.

For instance, Kodak's movie-camera business never really took off. With each new version, Kodak found that sales were consistent with the amount that was projected at a higher point on the curve, as if it were the original product continuing its life cycle. When sales were peaking quickly and then declining immediately after announcement of a new version at points on the tail end of the life-cycle curve, Kodak decided to get out of the business.

Life cycles of technology, just as product life cycles, offer a basis for a portfolio analysis of technology projects or a research and development program. One could begin by paraphrasing the Rogers stages of evolution as exploration, emergence, growth, early maturity, and late maturity for technologies. As the knowledge about a new technology increases, so does the level of worldwide project activity and interest. An example of this phenomenon has been the level of activity in superconductivity in the years since 1985. Each project increases the potential that spawns new projects. Within each technology one could create mini-life-cycle curves that reflect that portion that -is being explored versus the area that has been mined with the majority of applications defined.

Many technology companies do life-cycle analysis. Un-

---

* "Communication of Innovations," Everett M. Rogers with F. Floyd Shoemaker, The Free Press, New York, pp. 182–185.

fortunately, this is not carried over into the analysis of new products and businesses. Part of its value is in determining the skills needed in product development for both the long term and the short term. Projecting costs of product development and handling develop-and-make or buy decisions can be simplified with this approach.

HOW DOES IT GET DONE?

The scope of screening and evaluation, excluding monitoring, need not be exhausting or exhaustive. It is a matter of laying out the boundaries of the picture that will be developed and seeing whether all the pieces fit, whether the key issues are addressed, and whether the parts can work together so that a successful business operation can materialize.

Once a proposal has been sorted into the "yes" pile, venture capitalists try to learn as much as possible about the industry the business will be in, as well as the potential business itself. Much of this information comes from sources such as Dataquest, Creative Strategies, and other market research reports, and industry associations. They also call friends, consultants, and other venture capitalists for an initial understanding of the technology, the business's flaws, and the potential management. They may also call suppliers, clients for the product, and banks, to get their feelings. Venture capitalists rarely have problems getting information when they ask questions of people in the industry, even if the information is for a potential competitor.

Of course, this situation is sensitive in some companies. One extremely capable market analyst was accused of trading information because he seemed to have information that was "too good." Supposedly, he could not have gotten it unless he had "traded." In fact, he had the same sources as everyone else, but he also had the ability to interpret the information and come up with trends and conclusions that made it appear as if he had an inside track.

The road between academia and industry is also well worn, and perhaps more so by venture capitalists. Academics benefit by keeping in touch with the newest technology applications through their interactions with the venture capitalists. In some cases, professors are limited partners in venture-capital partnerships, lending their expertise to the investment decisions in an organized way and taking a limited partner's share of profits.

Key information sources may be actual or, in the case of a start-up, potential customers. The venture capitalist tries to find out what problems users of the product have encountered, what they liked and disliked about it, why they bought it and whether they would buy it again. Every problem addressed by a customer is investigated in detail, since it might be the flaw that would eventually jeopardize the venture's success.

HOW LONG SHOULD IT TAKE?

The character of the assessment phases is indicated by the time taken to accomplish them.

The decision as to whether a potential venture should be pursued to the screening phase can and should be made in a very short time—certainly in a morning or an afternoon. Some decisions can be made in five minutes.

The first screening—which should take less than half a

day—should address some of the highlights and key issues. In the second screening—which can take one to two full days—the analyst should be able to complete a full overview of the proposal.

A full-blown evaluation can take six weeks to six months, depending on the nature of the venture.

All of these estimates are time applied directly to the evaluation. The actual time spent will depend on the analyst's knowledge, the number of proposals he is handling, and the amount and quality of information that has been supplied by the proposal's author.

Chapter Four

The Business Plan

This chapter is concerned with the dynamics of the business plan: what it is supposed to do, the perspective of the entrepreneur in preparing this key document, and the perspective of the evaluator in looking at it.

It deals with the mechanics and content of business plans only as necessary, because many books have been written about business plans. One could pick up books such as *The Arthur Young Business Plan Guide*, by Eric Siegel et al.,* or *Building Your Business Plan*, by Harold J. McLaughlin.† Most, if not all, books on business plans provide outlines and discuss in detail the nature of each section of the plan and how to prepare it. The focus here is on the business plan as it relates to starting a new venture and keeping it going.

A poorly prepared plan makes it easier for the evaluator to find the inconsistencies and inaccuracies. These problems also make it more difficult to identify a good idea.

---

* John Wiley and Sons, Inc., 1987.
† John Wiley and Sons, Inc., 1985.

A good business plan states facts and explains assumptions, but is above all designed to excite the potential investor. To some extent, the evaluator must discount this emotional element in analyzing the merits of a potential venture. On the other hand, no one should recommend or decide to invest in a venture they are not excited about.

Only when a plan is the best possible document can it do justice to the idea, get the company's attention, and receive a favorable evaluation. Therefore, the entrepreneur needs to know how to package the idea from the perspective of the corporate evaluator.

In a corporation, the entrepreneur will have to present his idea to many executives. They sit as de facto multiple evaluators, and the corporate entrepreneur must also know how to handle that phase of marketing the proposal. Presentation technique is critically important in the corporate world.

As important as it is for the corporate entrepreneur to understand the corporation, the corporation must understand the psyche of the entrepreneur and how the plan was constructed.

WHAT IS A BUSINESS PLAN?

The business plan is the starting point for the relationship between the entrepreneur—corporate or independent—and the investor, whether a corporation, venture capital fund or private individual. The business plan is a written description of the proposed venture. It includes, among other things, the reasons why the business will be successful, a proposed financial measure of success, and the return the investors can expect on their investment.

It is also a game plan, explaining to the reader how a venture will get "there"—success—from "here"—the idea.

As the first form of contact between the entrepreneur and the investor, the business plan is an extension of the entrepreneur. In the corporate setting, this may be the first time the employee is presenting himself to the company as an entrepreneur. How the entrepreneur is perceived usually colors an investor's and executive's receptivity to the idea.

In the corporation, the business plan comes in two formats: as a complete document and as a summary presentation. As a rule, presentations are the vehicle for communications at the executive level.

WHY A BUSINESS PLAN?

Many new entrepreneurs believe that the business plan has only one function: to sell the idea and obtain the necessary funding. But the business plan also functions as a planning document and a measuring document.

The Funding Decision

The decision to fund a project means that people can be transferred to the project, equipment obtained, purchase orders approved for other equipment and materials, and facilities for offices and laboratories set aside.

But this happens only at the end of a long, tortuous process of reviews and presentations. In the corporate world the entrepreneur will probably have to present the idea to a lot of people before a cent is ever invested. Most companies don't have formal groups for pursuing venturing, and most of the people who will hear or read about the idea will not have a direct role in making the ultimate decision.

Although companies know that their futures may depend on new businesses, they still take a long time to act. Since corporate management is concerned with avoiding risk and since it has staff support available, many people may be asked for their input. Some executives will want friends and associates whose opinions they respect to review the business plan. Even the hottest idea will take a long time to come to fruition.

For every company that has established a streamlined way for handling new ideas and ventures, there are hundreds that have not. But regardless of a company's approach for selecting new ventures, the basis for evaluation is the business plan.

Planning

As a planning document, the business plan can be used by the entrepreneur and investor to test a number of "what-if" situations, both by calculating possible outcomes on paper and then, if one of those "what-ifs" is chosen as the way to proceed, by checking to see how well the outcome was predicted when the planning period is over.

In developing the business plan, the entrepreneur should continually test his original assumptions and question whether the resulting venture still "hangs together." Can all the events as described occur with the available resources and input, and will the projected results be realized?

Measuring

If the venture is undertaken, the business plan is essential as the basis for monitoring and measuring the achievement of milestones. Most plans are changed substantially by the time the business gets started, so it is useful to know what everyone expected at the outset, and why the plan was changed.

In addition, business plans should be prepared or updated at least annually, not just at the beginning of a business's life, since a comparison of the predictions from one year's business plan with the actual figures from that year can be used to create a data base for better forecasts.

WHO READS THE BUSINESS PLAN AND WHY?

Before writing any article or report, the writer must know who the audience will be and how this audience will use the information. In preparing a business plan, entrepreneurs must understand that the corporate reader will probably be someone assigned to evaluate the proposed venture rather than an investment manager/evaluator. Although entrepreneurs will have their own ideas as to what is important for the evaluation, they must be aware of what the evaluator will be looking for.

The independent entrepreneur sends a business plan usually to individuals, those able either to invest or to put him or her in touch with investors. The corporate entrepreneur either leaves the business plan with an executive who has been briefed on his venture or, more likely, will be asked to provide it to staff personnel to review. These staff evaluators have the advantage of detachment since the money at risk is not their own. However, by the same token, corporate evaluators will be less emotional and possibly less conscientious than independent venture capitalists might be. Corporate staff personnel will not be looking for "exciting" ventures, but rather for data to analyze and present to management.

In most companies the staff evaluators have a financial background. As would be expected, their concerns relate to the financial aspects of a proposal: investment, profits, and return on investment. They will explore the nature of the opportunity, the product, market appeal, and proprietary leverage. But their ability to integrate all of the information and analyze the proposal as a business rather than as several sets of numbers depends on their general analytical ability. This is the reality, although we recommend the permanent establishment of a special group to analyze new-business proposals. The venture professional will be more likely than the corporate evaluator to look at a plan in the context of a total operation, of which the financial aspects are only one part.

Those who analyze the business plan in a corporate environment will have a corporate orientation and will be used to working within the system. They will have a defined area of work and are likely to be conservative. They will be concerned about the company's vulnerability, and anything that creates a dramatic risk will not be well received. They will look for hidden risks. To some degree they will be willing to trade off risk for income and profits. In any event, the financial data will be extensively analyzed and contingency factors applied.

Most pricing analysts for large companies have limited knowledge of technical development and production processes. They build in contingency factors in part to compensate for their lack of knowledge. However, the major reason for contingency allowances is that these analysts have experienced many times that a particular project has not turned out as predicted, resulting in higher costs for the investing company.

Financial people are skeptical by nature and training. They also have long memories. A financial participant at a recent commemorative event for an entrepreneurial employee read a letter recalling "ventures I have known." He wrote:

> . . . projects abounded after they turned you loose. . . . My job at the time was to put some sanity into the proposals. I felt like a detective trying to stop you from playing with your machine. . . . I had a very difficult time convincing financial management that you did not own shares in [a non-profit collaborator] and secondly, that you intended on making a profit sometime during the strategic plan.*

THE READER'S OBJECTIVES

The reader of a business plan has four basic objectives when looking over a plan. They are:

- Understand the proposal
- Determine what is unique and why it is unique
- Determine the quality of the entrepreneur and his management team

---

* From a private letter.

• Decide whether to continue consideration of the proposal

If any of these objectives cannot be met, the onus should be placed on the plan's preparer to redo, recompute, or rethink the plan and present it again in a form that makes it possible for the reviewer to meet the objectives.

PREPARING THE BUSINESS PLAN

Both corporate and independent venture capitalists want to see a proposed venture presented as a fully developed idea with a complete business plan. While many entrepreneurs use consultants, accountants, or attorneys to help them prepare their business plans, the entrepreneur is ultimately responsible for producing a comprehensive plan.

In the corporate environment, entrepreneurs are on their own unless the company operates in the 3M mode. At 3M, all professional employees are considered potential entrepreneurs. They are authorized to "bootleg" time for new ventures and to obtain support. Essentially, they have to sell their ideas internally to obtain credibility. If the corporate entrepreneur is technically oriented and can find marketing and financial professionals to work with, the three of them should have most of the skills needed to prepare a plan.

Corporations with new-venture teams have in-house the expertise to create comprehensive business plans. This expertise should be exploited to encourage the submission of as many ideas as possible.

Most ideas proposed by first-time corporate entrepreneurs are neither well formulated nor well structured.

They lack the substance necessary for the venture group to determine whether the company should consider the proposed business. After determining that the proposed venture passes the initial sorting phase, the venture team should find a way to assist entrepreneurs in developing their ideas into business plans.

But the corporate venture team must set limits as they help these embryonic entrepreneurs develop their ideas. If team members become too involved in creating the business plan, there is the danger that they will compromise their subsequent roles as evaluators.

One natural resources company had a new-business team whose job was to come up with new ventures. If they came up with one that management selected, the venture team member working on that opportunity would get to head it. This was a strong incentive for the team to do a lot of work on the business plan as well as the evaluation. The problem with this approach is that the evaluator's desire to head up the new venture can warp an evaluation.

The best way to support corporate entrepreneurs may be to assign one member of the venture business to be the "champion" for each idea. That person will become, in effect, the consultant who works with an entrepreneur to develop the idea into a full-fledged venture proposal complete with business plan.

The amount of advocacy that champions are allowed to take for their "clients" can be determined by the members of the venture business. Some businesses allow advocates to argue the merits of their clients' cases, while others insist that entrepreneurs make their own presentations to the evaluating team.

All members of the venture business should have a portfolio of clients whom they are helping to develop plans, as well as a portfolio of other plans for which they are doing the primary screening and evaluation.

THE BUSINESS PLAN ITSELF

The business plan has a number of sections to it. Each one should give a comprehensive picture of a particular piece of the proposed venture. Key sections would include

- The overview or general description of the venture
- The venture's products and services
- The venture's marketing plan
- The venture's operational plan
- The venture's management and organizational structure
- The major milestones the venture will strive to achieve
- The venture's detailed financial plan
- The venture's financial structure and capitalization requirements (if appropriate, depending on the organizational relationship with the corporation).

There are a number of guidelines for preparing a business plan:

1. Criteria—Know the evaluator's and the company's criteria for evaluating and investing in a project and address them in the business plan.
2. Conservatism—Be realistic. If the market is unclear, the corporate entrepreneur may be overly optimistic. Attempt to size up the market realistically. Ultimately the evaluator must make the projection.

3. Consistency—The points made in each section must support one another and be consistent. For example, a product feature described as labor saving and encouraging widespread use of the product cannot be overlooked in calculating market size and sales.
4. Competence—The corporate entrepreneur must show a knowledge of the idea, the underlying technology, its applications, and customer receptivity.
5. Certainty—Neither corporate management nor investors like surprises. The risks must be stated clearly wherever they are applicable.
6. Completeness—All aspects of the venture should be addressed in the business plan.
7. Clarity—The business plan should be clearly written. If the business plan is too confusing, an investor may not take the time to read it and may reject it.
8. Coherence—The different aspects of the venture must hang together so that the objective of a viable venture can be met. See further discussion on viability in the chapter on screening and evaluation.
9. Comfort—Both the evaluator and the investing company must feel comfortable with the entire proposition. The foregoing guidelines will support this objective.

The General Description

This section of the business plan, which is usually only a few paragraphs in length, should give the reader a few key facts about the business. What is the business: manufacturing, distributing, retailing? Who generated the idea? What is his or her entrepreneurial and management record?

What are the business's goals, and what is the proposed time frame for their achievement?

The Products and Services

In this section, the business's particular products or services should be described in terms of their physical description, their applications, and their unique appeal. This section should also address the state of development of the product/service with some chronology of major events up to this point. This part of the plan will prepare the executive and evaluator for the scope of the development task and the level of investment required.

The Marketing Plan

In the marketing plan the entrepreneurs discuss how they intend to deal with current market forces, whether reacting to changes in the market or developing a new market for the particular product or service. The marketing plan is critical in "selling" the plan to investors, whether private or corporate.

The marketing plan must deal with four specific areas:

1. *The definition of the market and opportunities within the market.* The marketing plan must establish that there is a need and demand for the product. If other products, especially less expensive ones, serve the same purpose, the question is, What makes this product or service so special? Some products will also have a secondary market. Where the demand in both the primary and the secondary markets is expected to be the same, the corporate entrepreneur should select one or the other as the near-term target. Both markets should be spelled out, and companies should not

overemphasize the primary market at the expense of the secondary market. Sometimes the secondary market eventually becomes the primary market.

When collagen was first developed, the company and venture-capitalist backers intended to market the product for the treatment of burn cases. Collagen is a natural constituent of connective tissue, and the company had found a way for stimulating the body's development of the tissue to repair burn damage to the body. The difficulty of entering the hospital market was offset when the developers found a niche in the cosmetics industry. As a cosmetic, collagen is promoted as a "fill-in" to mask the effects of acne and scars.

Another case in which the secondary market became primary involves the personal computer, which was originally created for the individual and home market. Although the business market was viewed as a secondary market, this turned out to be much larger, and more near-term.

2. *The world of competition.* Competition is more than just another company or product. It is the total set of influences that affect a customer's decision to buy a specific product. Consumer behavior is influenced not only by products and their advertising, but also by current fads and peer influences. Ignoring these external factors would create an incomplete picture of the business opportunity.

The marketing plan must also address the question of how much influence competition will have on the projected growth of the proposed business. Other important influences include changing patterns in consumer habits and possible changes in government regulation of the industry involved.

3. *The marketing strategy.* The range of tools that can be used as part of the marketing strategy includes advertising,

public relations, and specialized market support. Most entrepreneurs, particularly corporate entrepreneurs, are not conversant with a broad range of marketing techniques. However, they should spell out any particular angle or product feature that might be exploited to improve marketing success.

4. *A sales forecast.* The sales forecast could be in terms of the overall market potential, the number of customers that might have particular need for the product, or the number that could be sold in a particular geographic area. Specific information regarding market segmentation or the size of the market enables the evaluator to do a better job and increases the probability that the company will select the proposed venture for development.

It is also worthwhile to summarize the sales information that will appear in the detailed financial plan and to include that summary in the marketing plan so it can be seen in the proper context. The results of any market research should also be included in the marketing plan section, although some of this information and its implications will find its way into other parts of the business plan. Some entrepreneurs devote a separate section of the business plan to market research.

The Operational Plan

The operational plan explains how the venture will actually create the goods or services it will be selling. Such issues as manufacturing, materials, labor, and vendor relations need to be addressed in this section. The operational plan should describe how the corporate entrepreneur will transform the idea and the current level of development into a finished product or service. This plan should enumerate the tasks and resources necessary, and propose a timetable for the completion of major stages. This kind of detail brings reality to a great idea.

The operational section also serves as the basis for an internal planning document and for establishing benchmarks by which to measure progress during the period of performance. The time frame for the operational-plan portion should continue beyond the point when the product has entered the market, and should describe the ancillary support and services that will be offered to customers. This is worthwhile only if market entry is fairly close-in and reasonable estimates can be made of potential expenses. At the very least, if customer support is a key ingredient in the marketing strategy, it should be described in general terms.

As we have said, corporations are averse to risk, avoiding risk whenever possible. Venture capitalists, on the other hand, try to manage risk. They accept that there is risk in every situation and that they may lose their entire investment. With these facts in mind, independent entrepreneurs who have been through the process know that they must identify major potential risks.

The chapter on assessment talked about "fatal flaws," the handful or so of items that could prevent the product from reaching the market. Problem areas could include having a sole-source supplier for a critical part, incorporating a new technology into the product, or a servicing issue that has not been addressed. Perhaps the product is so unique that direct marketing may be needed to get sales started, but the level of investment and the profit margin will not permit this marketing effort to continue for very long. There may be some operational considerations that are out of the entrepreneur's control, such as government regulation of the industry in question. These potential problems should all be dealt with in detail in the business plan so that there will be no surprises later on. Plans to overcome potential "deal breakers" should be outlined.

The operational plan is also the place to describe any problems relating to the proprietary position of the business's patents, trademarks, copyrights, or licenses.

Management and Organizational Structure

In this section, the entrepreneur should describe the major organizational components required to manage the business, specific skills management will need to run this venture, and any particular candidates recommended for management positions.

This part of the plan has two key areas:

- **An organizational chart,** which lays out the key functions in the business, even if the people who will fulfill those functions are not yet known. In some instances, a number of organizational charts are used to show how the business's functional divisions will change over time as more staff is added.
- **A discussion of the management team,** which may be long or short, depending on whether the company's management wants the ultimate decision as to who will manage the new business or whether the venture business team and the entrepreneur can put together their own team.

If executive management intends to name a corporate entrepreneur to head the venture, it may accept recommendations for other management slots. Corporate managements who are more serious about venturing usually let the entrepreneur, or a "champion" who has worked with the entrepreneur, head the venture and pick his or her own team.

Many corporate executives tend to choose a "corporate type" who may have difficulty managing the venture. For the most part, the people brought in by top management are interested in the business, work hard, but lack "entrepreneurial" characteristics.

As one representative said of people who manage new ventures for his company, they lack the necessary commitment. He made the point that the more exotic or esoteric the business, the greater the required commitment. Top management of a non-technical company cannot treat a technical venture as a "plain vanilla" business. They have to get into the details of the business and "get grubby." In large corporations, executives often come to ventures because they are on a "fast track," and management uses the venture opportunity to season them without major exposure to the corporation. Unfortunately, the ventures suffer.

Outside of the corporate environment, the management section is one of the first areas a reviewer will turn to. Venture capitalists place a lot of faith in their intuition about people, and many consider their real investment to be in people rather than in products, services, or concepts.

Major Milestones

Major milestones provide the best way to measure the business's progress. They also give potential investors—in this case the corporation's venture business—an idea of whether the proposed venture fits into the corporation's time frame for payback and return.

Milestones are usually a key element in the technical plan. They tell management when to expect certain accomplishments. When extensive development is required for a new product, the milestones become more critical.

Milestones should be noted in general terms in this section of the plan and keyed to the financing commitment (in the corporate case the time when the venture actually commences, since the entrepreneur would not have been working officially on the project before seeking funding). Examples of milestones include a demonstration that key concepts work, the development and operation of prototypes, the first marketing tests, the initiation of production and sales, the point where financial "break-even" is attained, and the points at which expansions will occur or new products and/or services will be initiated.

The milestones that are noted should be clearly defined and measurable. The caveat is that the proposed time frame for meeting them should be ambitious but not unrealistic. Ventures almost always take longer to pan out than anticipated. Entrepreneurs tend to overstate their hand in the area of milestones, and a venture-business team that is working hand-in-hand with the entrepreneur can eliminate much of the "brinkmanship" that goes on when it comes to establishing realistic milestones.

The Financial Plan

This is, in many ways, the meat and potatoes of a business plan, the part where the entrepreneur, using all available information, projects a comprehensive and credible set of financial results for the venture. These line items address the source and application of funds for the venture and the resulting income. Everyone who reads a business plan should understand that the projections reflect only a guess, since there is no historical data to back them up, but they must get the sense that the entrepreneur is at least defining things that exist in the real world.

In setting forth financial projections, the entrepreneur must explain them with the relevant assumptions. When there are several likely scenarios (best case, most likely outcome, worst case), the financial outcome of all three should be projected.

Most start-ups take much more time and money than anticipated. The estimate for first-stage start-ups is usually wrong, not only because the entrepreneur understates his needs, but also because there are few facts to work with.

If technology is involved, much effort will be required to ensure that a product configuration will work, that it can be packaged appropriately, and that the human engineering aspects have been adequately considered.

Estimates of costs and market potential are also likely to be wrong because the corporate entrepreneur does not usually have much background in the diverse aspects of a business operation. If he has worked for a long time in the corporate environment, he will lack knowledge about a number of important areas because of corporate compartmentalization. He is also likely to neglect allowances for furniture and fixtures, costs per square foot of space, and tools, because "the company has them."

The Structure and Capitalization

If the venture is an independent start-up, financial structure and capitalization are an important part of the business plan. By definition, the corporate venture will be structured as a part of the parent company. But companies today may have different thoughts regarding their venturing activities. They may be considering the establishment of subsidiaries and other organizational structures in which the entrepreneurs could participate financially. These alternatives would provide incentives for entrepreneurs and key members of the venture. In any event, funding is dependent on the nature of the organization. (Funding corporate ventures will be discussed in a separate chapter.) The venture's capital requirements must be clearly defined and agreed upon from the start.

PRESENTATION

A critical skill for both corporate entrepreneurs and corporate evaluators is the ability to package the venture for presentation. Although independent entrepreneurs may have occasional need for presentations, this tool is essential in the corporation.

Corporate executives do not have time to read lengthy documents, which are instead given to staff people to review, digest, tear apart, and analyze. As a result, the decisions for new ventures in companies are often made by executives who have familiarity with only the project's high points.

The corporate entrepreneur should be directly involved in presenting the venture idea. Otherwise, important elements may not receive appropriate emphasis. Also, the enthusiasm factor, critical for executive approval, is lost. A staff person can't be expected to display the same level of emotion as an entrepreneur.

Executive Presentation Format

The purpose of the presentation is to offer highlights and meaningful detail to the evaluating executive. For example, the financial projections need only be shown in aggregate form by year for all major functions. Detail for each line item projected for five or more years is needless.

The presentation should include the same sections covered in the business plan. An informative tone will encourage a receptive attitude from the executive. Too often entrepreneurs come across as arrogant, or concerned only with the idea, leaving the business aspects of the venture to others. Finally, enthusiasm is contagious.

Chapter Five

The New-Business Charter

Before a corporation can begin the process of searching out, evaluating, and developing potential new-business ventures, it must develop and commit in writing to a new-business charter.

Without a charter a company can end up in the situation of one company, which after years of venturing on an ad-hoc basis, tried to explain changes in its management system by writing: "The experience obtained in operating these units reveals a lack of progress by many in achieving their plans, changes in direction and plans without top management understanding. . . ."

WHAT IS THE CHARTER?

The charter is, in effect, a contract that defines the terms and conditions under which the new-venture business will be conducted and the roles various players will play in the venturing process. The charter addresses three basic relationships:

The New-Business Charter

1. Most important, the charter is an agreement that the corporation makes with itself defining the parameters of its new-business venturing operations. The charter should outline the structure the new-venture business will take, how the new-venture business will be conducted, the time-frame and financial commitment for investments, and a host of other variables.

2. The charter is also an agreement between the corporation and the new-venture business management explaining the rights and responsibilities of the new-venture business with regard to finding and developing new businesses for the corporation.

3. The charter is a three-way agreement among the corporation, the new-venture business, and each individual new business; the charter outlines the relationships among the three entities with regard to each new business. These relationships will vary greatly, depending on how the new-venture business is designed; for instance, the charter determines whether the new-venture business will merely turn over candidates for start-up to senior management, or whether it will help set up management teams and act as a fiduciary for the corporation, as a venture capitalist does for his investors.

Commitment

The charter is also a document that defines commitment—what it is and who has it.

In defining commitment, we will use the same definition used by venture capitalists when they talk to entrepreneurs who are requesting funding. A conversation might go something like this:

vc: What are you putting into the deal?

e: My knowledge and my time.

vc: And what else?

e: I'll work hard, at least 80 hours a week; and it's my idea.

vc: And?

e: I really want this to succeed.

vc: But how much money are you investing?

Commitment is the total emotional and material investment in a deal. Corporate management has the tendency not to worry or be concerned with details. Management can operate this way with an established business because most people understand the dynamics, at least implicitly. However, with a new style of operation, management cannot take the details for granted. Not only is management unfamiliar with the operation, but so are other company personnel.

Very often, the problems management has with its venturing program derive from conflicting emotions, some of them not well founded. Management's understanding and knowledge may be clear at the outset. However, over time the clarity, crispness, and content get fuzzy. When confronted with reality, unrealized expectations can lead to vacillation and shifts in the ground rules for venturing.

The venturing charter is all about commitment: laying the groundwork for it, defining it, and making sure everyone understands it, especially management. All contracts, including the venturing charter, are valuable because they lay out the terms and conditions of the transaction. Contracts force the parties to think through the entire arrangement, and to anticipate the ramifications of their plans. A contract is usually prepared before people get emotionally involved and before emotions get distorted by events.

Consistency

Another major benefit of the charter is that it forces a test for internal consistency. The charter should answer such questions as:

- Is the company going into venturing in order to extend its expertise in either products or markets, or is the company seeking real diversification by looking for both new products and new markets?
- How much money is the corporation going to put into the venturing effort? How many new businesses would it like to start with that money? And how long a period will the new-venture business have to invest the money?

The charter contract and the strategy for the new-venture business must be compatible. In fact, the charter is in part derived from the new-venture strategy, just as parts of the implementation plan are obtained from the charter.

THE OBJECTIVES OF VENTURING

The first item a corporation must consider when drawing up a new-business venture charter is the corporation's objective for getting into venturing in the first place.

In the traditional venture-capital firm there is a single objective: capital gains. To achieve that objective, venture capitalists operate independently, and their investors are willing to let them pursue their own intuitions and activities. There may be board meetings and other means of keeping the investors informed, but in most cases the venture capitalists make it clear that they will make decisions unilaterally. Of course, in part their independence and freedom are derived from a successful track record.

Although there is no active internal corporate-venturing operation that we can use as a model, there are corporate venture-capital groups. But even in these cases, their objectives are not as clearly defined as they should be, and they are often poorly implemented. Although many companies may say their principal objective is long-term capital gains, this objective becomes confused with other objectives and at times may even be subordinated to the other objectives.

Exxon sponsored a number of ventures under its Exxon Enterprises. The businesses in this group were concerned with advanced office systems, and many of the ventures funded were compatible with these activities. When Exxon began acquiring some of its ventures, it was satisfying an objective other than capital gains, and entrepreneurs became frightened because they felt that in the process of being acquired, their particular company would not achieve the net worth for which they had originally gone into business.

One corporate venture-capital group said that all of its investments must fit in with company strategy, creating and supporting its own competition by establishing and fostering small businesses. If a new company can build up its technology, the parent company may then have a market for licensing the capability.

Another corporate venture capitalist said that his company's original objective was to create a window on technology; however, that has since shifted, and capital gains is now the primary objective. This seems to be the pattern for most corporate venture-capital groups.

In contrast to the company previously cited, most companies will not fund their competition. One corporate venture capitalist said that he looks inside the company for attractive ventures that have become part of the company "out" plan, highly desirable projects for which there are no resources. This company offers the developers of these unfunded projects the opportunity to become entrepreneurs, although a prospective entrepreneur must sever all connections with the company.

The corporation must decide the development stage of its start-up projects: prototype, development, or seed. If the goal is to start a number of businesses, management must decide how the portfolio will be structured. Will there be businesses in all three stages? Will the parameters of the portfolio be defined by the number of businesses in each stage, the total investment in businesses in each stage, or the percentage of anticipated revenue over a certain time period that will be produced by businesses at each stage?

Prototype projects are those that are usually two to three years away from commercialization, with demonstrated feasibility of the product and state-of-the-art technology. The market is often in place, and the focus is on preparing and packaging the product for the marketplace.

Development projects are about four to seven years away from commercialization, and require some advances in the state of the art. The market in these cases is rarely well defined.

Seed projects are usually eight to 10 years away from commercialization, and require significant breakthroughs in technology and understanding of the potential market.

Each stage has its own risks and potentials, and the corporate executives who develop the charter must decide just how much they want to risk with each type of business.

THE VENTURE BUSINESS'S DURATION

If the new-venture business is being set up along the lines of a venture-capital fund, it should probably be set up for a duration of between 10 and 15 years, taking into account the fact that good ideas cannot be programmed, the time that projects will need to reach commercialization, and the years after commercialization before reaching profitability. It may take as long as five years for the fund to be fully invested, which involves finding enough worthwhile ideas. As we have said, corporate start-ups usually take between seven and eight years to get into the black, compared with under four years for independent start-ups.

In calculating the duration of the new-venture business, management must also consider the mix of projects and the different stages of development that will postpone the break-even date for some of them. And, of course, there is also the fact that some of the businesses will fail. Venture capitalists say that in some cases one can know whether a venture will be successful in about two and one-half years, even though it still may be five years away from turning a profit.

FINANCING

Decisions about objectives and duration of the new-venture business go hand-in-hand with decisions about how the new businesses will be funded. There are many alternatives.

Funding ventures is not something corporate management feels comfortable with. Many corporate people who are involved in setting up a 15-year venture business will not be around to see the fruits of their labor. Therefore, the venture business may not enhance one's career, and could even adversely affect it if all or a large part of the investment is lost.

But funding is an integral part of the new-venture business. Will the new-venture business be given a total fund, or pool, to invest? Will it have guidelines on how to invest? Will the venture business make recommendations on funding and then turn over budget authority to the corporate level? If so, will the corporate budget makers in effect set up a bank account to draw on for each new business, letting the managers draw on their own accounts? Will funding be based on progress—with each new business required to reach milestones—in order to get continued funding? Or will the new business have to go to the corporate budget makers repeatedly in order to fund major budget items?

As the final financial element of the charter, executive management must set its financial goal for the new-venture business as a whole. A conservative estimate may be 20 percent compounded annually, the return sought by Small Business Investment Companies (SBICs) affiliated with banks, which are generally far more conservative in their estimates and their risk-taking than are private venture-capital partnerships.

Financial Management

Prudent financial management dictates taking a portfolio approach, diversifying the projects in terms of products, markets, and stages of business development. Not all funding should be put into the same type of business. Keep in mind that most business-plan cost estimates are low and do not provide for contingencies. Therefore, two-thirds to three-quarters of the money allocated for the investment fund should be invested according to the business plans presented, with one-quarter to one-third of the fund withheld for contingencies and "supplemental" funding of projects that either underestimate their needs or run into problems along the way.

Funding for the Long Term

Management must take a long-term view in funding the business because the total investment takes place over several years. Since companies budget and fund annually, management must provide for and ensure long-term continuity of funding for its ventures. The tendency in most companies is for the venture management to begin hiring people (either internally or from the outside), obtain fairly nice facilities, nice furniture, and so on. Independent entrepreneurs generally do not think of such luxuries. Their focus is on getting the business rolling, and there is an element of sacrifice rarely seen in corporate halls. Moreover, most companies don't include facilities, furniture, and fixtures in the financing numbers, so that real investment requirements end up being understated.

Successful investments require more capital than failures. Things can be moving along, and milestones achieved, but an unexpected problem or new situation may require additional funding. The investing corporation must be prepared for this possibility.

Costs of Managing

No matter how the corporation decides to manage its venturing effort, it must consider management-related costs as part of its investment. To avoid overstaffing the new-venture unit, personnel costs associated with finding and developing new ventures should be pegged at a fixed percentage of the total new-venture fund. Venture capitalists once again provide a good guideline for this—they charge a "management fee" of about 3 to 5 percent on "smaller" funds of under $10 million, and 1.5 to 2 percent on larger funds, up to about $30 million. The costs of managing a $30 million fund are not substantially greater than those of running a $10 million fund.

MANAGEMENT AND CONTROLS

The relationship between corporate management and the management of the new-venture business must be clearly defined. Management must decide on the extent of its involvement, from the minimum—attendance at the annual dinner celebrating the successes of the new-venture business management—to the maximum—semimonthly meetings and passing judgment on all investments. Management may want to set a threshold for investment in ventures, above which it wants to have some input, if not the final decision, and below which the new-venture business unit has carte blanche.

Active or Passive Management?

Possibly the most critical decision corporate management will make in drawing up the management portion of the charter is whether corporate management will assume the position of a passive investor in these new businesses or whether it will be an active manager of each new business when it is created. This decision may be the most difficult part of defining the relationship. Management may try to change the rules in the middle of the game. After initially agreeing to an arm's-length relationship, management may decide it needs more control if it believes money is being spent casually.

Many senior executives may be loath to give up control over new businesses, preferring to bring them into the company in the traditional way as divisions or units of divisions. Others may feel that to start a number of new businesses will drain management time and effort, and they would rather put the money aside in an investment pool and think of it as being managed by outsiders, even if those outsiders are people from within the company.

Regardless of management's decision about who will have hands-on responsibility for managing the new businesses, the corporation must be willing to make a number of commitments to the new-venture business in order for it to be successful. Management must be willing to provide specific strategic guidance that expands on its general objectives. It must be willing to offer specific counsel on how to achieve these objectives, yet at the same time be willing to admit that the new-venture unit will over time develop its own sense of how to reach management's objectives. In addition, the corporation must set up a rational and workable reporting relationship with the new-venture unit. Making the rules up as the situation goes along just will not work.

Inherent Conflict

There is an inherent potential for conflict between management and the people who run new-venture units. The conflict runs something like this: if the new-venture business is staffed with entrepreneurial people, aggressive individuals who can search out and evaluate the best possible ventures, they will have a tendency to go off on their own. They may not be conscientious about providing management with information about where the venture business is going, which can lead to a situation where management either disagrees with the direction or simply feels angered by the apparent lack of communication. If, on the other hand, the unit is staffed with good corporate people, they may be afraid to make a move without going through the corporate-style decision-making process, through layers of management. Some members of management may get impatient with this arrangement, perceiving that the venture business is not going far enough fast enough.

The optimal situation is to have an entrepreneurially oriented new-venture business and, at the same time, a clear understanding about the extent of its responsibility to corporate management. There must be guidelines at the beginning of the process about how often the new-venture unit is to report to corporate management and the types of issues that should be brought to corporate management's attention. The corporation must also make sure those running the new-venture business have ready access to management. When entrepreneurial people run into a problem, their tendency will be to make the best decision possible themselves rather than wait days to discuss a problem with corporate management. The new-venture business must have a direct entrée into senior corporate management.

One way to accomplish this is to set up an advisory board of senior executives for the new-venture business. The advisory board would have "board of directors" powers over the venture business's activities, such as review and approval over major expenditures and final say over the decision to take a prospective business beyond evaluation and into development. This board should be directly responsible to the CEO.

PERFORMANCE MEASUREMENT

Knowing that corporate employees are looking for promotion and compensation, management must set up the basis for appraisal at the outset.

Harold Geneen says that intrapreneurship does not work because companies cannot afford to throw their compensation schedules into disarray with unreasonable and disproportionate salary increases. Yet with a carefully designed structure, both entrepreneurs and the new-venture business management can be rewarded in a manner consistent with corporate guidelines. Venture capitalists do not leave compensation up in the air, and neither should corporations.

At the outset, management should negotiate the terms of employment with the people who will serve as the new-venture business management. Compensation, bonuses, the basis for measuring performance, and other applicable terms and conditions must be included in this discussion.

Evaluation Criteria

There must also be a formalized process of review, monitoring, and evaluation of the new-venture management by the appropriate corporate executives. Although members of this new-venture business will not be asked to give up the security of working for a corporation, their compensation should be tied to performance, which can be evaluated by weighing a number of factors, among them:

- **Quality and quantity of ideas received.** In the first year or two this would take into account the development of a program encouraging the generation of ideas by employees, and the promotion of that program.
- **Quality of business analyses, research ability, and research skills.** In the beginning people with apparent research skills will join the new-venture business, but only in time will their abilities be demonstrated by their venture activities and the performance of their ventures.
- **Relationships with corporate management, others in the new-venture management, and individuals in the venture teams.** This is important to reinforce the need to communicate effectively and to maintain close working relationships with everyone involved in the venturing process.
- **Developing ideas into suitable businesses.**

If the management team for the new-venture business will have total responsibility for overseeing the new ventures, the team should be measured on three other criteria as well:

- **Management of the investment fund**
- **Quality of the businesses funded**
- **Progress of the businesses funded**

GETTING OUT

There will be individual ventures that go sour, but this alone should not cause termination of the venturing program. However, there could be unusual circumstances that would lead to a suspension or termination of venturing. The company should anticipate these when creating its charter.

In the contract, the corporation needs to discuss the terms under which it would dissolve the new-venture business. Admittedly, these are difficult issues. The contract may be written too tightly and thus dissuade anyone from coming on board to manage the new-venture business.

Management may not consciously constrain the effort when writing a contract to undertake venturing. Nevertheless, when they see what they might be agreeing to, there may be second thoughts about going ahead. Many companies also may not want to go through the time and negotiating necessary to produce a charter, preferring a "gentlemen's agreement," even though they might have undertaken a previous new-venture business that failed. In both cases, they would be undermining the potential future success of the venturing effort.

RELATIONSHIPS BETWEEN THE CORPORATION AND INDIVIDUAL NEW BUSINESSES

The primary focus of the charter is on the relationship between the corporate management and the new-venture business management. However, if corporate management decides to require approval of each investment and to handle the distribution of funds, it must make several other decisions with regard to its ongoing relationship with each new venture. For example:

- Who will be responsible for overseeing and monitoring the venture?
- Who will establish the ongoing relationships with venture managers and stand by to help when needed?

Management beset with day-to-day responsibilities and profit objectives may in time resent diverting time and energy from its prime responsibilities. The amount of effort needed to manage ventures is substantial. If we look at data from venture capitalists, we find that a venture capitalist can handle no more than six ventures at different stages at one time. An equal split among six projects would allow about 16 percent of the manager's time for each venture, and a venture in trouble might take as much as 25 or 30 percent of that person's time.

Monitoring refers to the process of keeping abreast of what is going on with a venture, and helping the venture group through difficult times. A good venture capitalist knows what is going on long before a problem gets to the critical point. This involves continually visiting the operation and talking frequently with management and personnel in the venture.

How many executives have the time to do this? How many executives can remain objective about a venture, without feeling like the game is "You Bet Your Company"? Corporate management should have a healthy "arm's-length" distance from the daily activities of the venture. The everyday responsibilities should be turned over to venture professionals, who must be given a considerable amount of discretion.

Chapter Six

Venture Shock

When company executives decide to engage in venturing, the organization often goes into "venture shock." Many of the individuals, and indeed many of the systems the company has developed and rewarded over the years, become traumatized by the perceptions and the fears of what the company will be like after venturing takes hold. At the heart of this venture shock are the differences between the cultures and operating styles of the venture and the ongoing business. The shock can be caused by something as radical as the changes in organization brought about by a venture, or by something as mundane as the distribution and sales channels that will be used.

For example, one company was well known as a producer of fine jewelry and watches sold through upscale retail jewelry outlets. In the early 1970s the company also had a military products division, an industrial products division, and a precision metals division. These divisions had totally different markets and different sales forces, selling directly to corporate users.

At this time the company was looking for new products

and markets to capitalize on. A brainstorming session with people from the industrial products division led to proposals for a series of consumer-oriented goods based on industrial products division technology. One was a timer for home use.

These products would be marketed through retail channels such as hardware stores and home improvement stores, and sold to them through distributors. The proposed distribution channels did not match any the company had used before. The products could be perceived as consumer items, but executives worried about how customers would relate these products to the goods sold at jewelry outlets. In addition, these products could cause jewelry customers and employees of the consumer divisions to wonder whether the company was going "downscale." Also, working in a new market area with little leverage would give them less control over the distribution system. Even though the venture promised to be profitable, the executives finally said, "We don't want to deal with those people."

The company's decision not to venture into this area of consumer retailing was based on valid concerns. Melding the cultures of many different businesses is one of the most difficult jobs for managers of multibusiness companies.

THE VENTURING DECISION

The decision to have a company go into venturing, perhaps more than the decision to go into a particular venture, can come as a shock to many of the people in the organization; they wonder whether management's time and energy will be so diverted by the ventures that it will spend less time thinking about or caring about the ongoing businesses. They may even start wondering whether in a few years the ongoing businesses will even be around, or whether they might all be allowed to wither and die.

One medium-sized company provides a medical service essentially without competition. Lack of aggressive and innovative management has, in the past, made stockholders unhappy. A new management was brought in and made changes in the marketing program, but also adopted a strategy of diversification through acquisitions.

Resources are being accumulated to complete acquisition of a company that is unrelated in core skills and abilities, although it is in the same general business area. This has been done despite the fact that customers have not perceived any changes in the company's products and services for at least 10 years. In this case, there may be a concern that employees see no indications that there will be any investment in the company's core business while the acquisition drive is going on.

The Impact on the Work Force

It is important to understand that venturing may be perceived as a trauma to many people in the work force. The company must work to calm their anxieties about what venturing will mean to them. They must be educated about what venturing is and what it isn't, and most of all what effect, if any, it will have on them. Company leaders must understand the culture of their company, and the organizational climate in which they work. They must anticipate the fears and concerns of company employees about venturing and be ready to deal with those concerns.

Preparing the work force is less of a problem in companies where the management and the orientation of the company is entrepreneurial. In companies such as these—the best-known is probably 3M—employees are always expecting that the company will be getting into something new. The work force and executives, having grown up in an environment where this is the rule rather than the exception, are always supportive. In fact, at any time many employees are involved in projects of their own, hoping their idea will be the next "Post-it," reflector, or overhead projector.

The 3M model is based on company entrepreneurs internally "selling" their ideas to others and "bootlegging time" to refine and develop their ideas. Also, since many corporate executives were former entrepreneurs, their spirit, culture, and values embody the characteristics of entrepreneurial change.

When companies are contemplating a move to venturing, company leaders must communicate to company employees that venturing is a positive, forward-looking activity, not only for the venture itself, but also for the entire company's future. The message must be that venturing provides growth not only at the company's perimeters, but within the company's core as well.

In order to implement a venturing program successfully, company executives must understand several key issues:

• The concerns of employees, and how those concerns are communicated.
• The types of behavior often shown toward ventures by employees of the mainline business.

- The reasons why these concerns and behaviors need to be addressed.
- The best communication medium with which to address those concerns.

EMPLOYEE CONCERNS

The first concern of most, if not all, employees is, Will I have a job next week?

When companies enter venturing, employees often feel threatened. They fear that the company is going to change drastically and that their expertise and competence may no longer be needed. They begin asking themselves, "Is there something I don't know about this company?" Some employees may fear that the style of a company will change significantly when venturing occurs.

Their questions are often couched in more short-term than long-term language: Will my pay be limited, especially in comparison with others in the company? Will the people in the ventures be compensated better than I? If the place becomes "leaner" and less hierarchical, will I, the middle manager, no longer be needed? If people are being brought in from the outside, what does that mean for my upward mobility? If the "best" people are being shifted to the ventures, will those not chosen be locked into areas of the business that will wither away?

EMPLOYEE BEHAVIOR

When employees are worried about their future, they may either consciously or unconsciously try to hinder the venturing program. For example, if the processing of paper-work for ventures is done within departments of the main business, it is not uncommon for employees to do the work of the venture last. The attitude may be part "This is not my main task," part "This is not the part of the company that earns profits and really makes it go," and part "This new venture could be threatening my existence in the future." This attitude can be contagious, and can drastically hurt momentum for a start-up.

CONCERN FOR THE ORGANIZATION

If there is discord among employees about venturing, the entire company will be hurt. The pressure during this period is on management, from all directions. On the one hand there is a new type of activity, or perhaps many new activities, with new markets, new products, and a new type of organization. At the same time, management must be concerned with the home base, making sure it functions smoothly and remains the same type of organization it has always been and that it continues to produce the profits that will deliver increased bonuses.

It will take a concerted communication effort to make sure all employees understand the philosophy of venturing, how venturing will work in the corporation, and the reasons why venturing is necessary to the corporation. Communication has four parts: the message, the messenger, the media, and the moment.

The message needs to be positive and consistent.

The moment for communication should arrive as early as is feasible, and information should keep flowing.

The media should be those that the company is comfortable with; this is not the time to add flashy new videos if the company has a 50-year-old weekly newspaper.

Every executive needs to be a messenger, demonstrating cohesiveness and support.

The Message

The message to employees must be positive: opportunity, position, and stability. It must stress to them that growth and diversification through venturing offer the best insurance that the company will continue to prosper.

Opportunity for everyone will be enhanced by venturing. Those who want a role in the venturing, who feel that being a part of the company's mainline business does not afford them enough opportunity to be creative and grow professionally, may find that opportunity in the new ventures. Those who are looking for more responsibility within the ongoing business will find that also.

Position will be enhanced for many people as the company expands. Rather than seeing growth only as vertical, going into supervisory, line-management, or top-management positions, managers can assume more responsibility as the company grows outward, without losing touch with the company's productive heart and soul.

Stability will be enhanced for all by assuring that the company continues to grow and prosper, that it grows horizontally and continues to establish firm footings in new business areas.

Employee Advantages

Venturing can bring added job security, although not necessarily in an employee's current job. Horizontal growth of the business, and the necessary shifts in the company's climate, can make each employee more valuable to the future company, and if certain areas of the company are phased out, employees could be absorbed by other areas of the company.

New ventures may compensate for revenue and profit fluctuations in the mature businesses, and can also serve as a hedge against market changes in the mature businesses. In addition, the new talent brought in during the venturing process adds new skills to the company, and can help enhance other employees' abilities. These may become the core skills for future company ventures.

Sharing Information

The message should be as specific as possible. There is no reason not to share information and ideas with employees. More important, companies must help employees understand the information.

Among the specific elements that need to be communicated are

- The business climate, current company sales and trends, the direction of the industry that the company is in, and the company's position within that industry. This lays the groundwork for an understanding of the business realities that the company must deal with. Often employees are not cognizant of trends or predictions relating to the industry and market that they work in. They may have some gut feelings, based on their perceptions of the general economy, how many people they see in stores buying company products, industry layoffs or furloughs, contract negotiations, or just reading the newspaper. But they are often not privy to the predictions being made in the front offices, as they should be. It is only within the context of business reality that they will see venturing as a logical step.

- The company's new direction, the reasons for it, and the objectives it hopes to reach. It is only after getting a firm grounding in business realities that the reasons for moving in a particular direction will make sense. The objectives should have time frames for achievement, so people understand that any change in corporate strategy and direction is gradual, and does not mean that they will not fit into the scheme.
- The nature of the new venture and how it will help implement the new direction the company wants to be going in. The specifics of the venture must be laid out clearly, including:

1. The venture business's organization and management, as well as the organization and management of individual ventures when they are created.
2. Staffing. What are the venture business's staff requirements, and the qualifications necessary? What will be the opportunities with each new venture? What is the application procedure? Will an employee's being chosen for a venture enhance position and promotion possibilities? What are the risks—is there the option to return to a previous job if the venture washes out?
3. The venture business's operating style, as well as the expected operating style of the new ventures.
4. How to interact with the venture business; how to submit ideas for consideration.

5. Changes that employees can expect to see, such as significant hiring from the outside or even retrenchment of some divisions.
6. The major interactions between the company and each new venture. To what extent will the new ventures be dependent on the company in terms of research, administrative support, and other areas?

Helping company personnel to interpret the information, especially as it affects their particular situation, is as critical as providing the information in the first place.

The Moment

Sudden change in large corporations creates problems in more ways than one. It takes little time for information to leak out. The rumor mill starts turning, and employees exaggerate stories they hear. Correct information and wrong information combine to create conclusions that should never have been drawn. How often have employees speculated on reorganizations that were never carried out—although they may have been considered—or that were not as far-reaching as speculated on? The reverberations of the rumor usually exceed the impact of any change; people take time from their work every day to speculate, and as the time when people believe something will happen gets closer without any official word, speculation increases and productivity decreases.

Obviously, an announcement cannot be made at the beginning of deliberations on venturing. However, as soon as it is practicable, complete information must be provided to allay concerns and to begin developing a cooperative atmosphere. The earliest point at which an announcement should be made is after the charter has been prepared and a plan for venturing has been formulated.

Although everyone in the organization should receive essentially the same information, that information should be packaged differently for different constituencies within the company, in terms that are most meaningful to them. An executive's understanding of his relationship with the company is very different from that of an hourly worker or first-line manager.

The preparation and communication of the message should be handled with the utmost care. Management must determine who is on what list to receive what level of detailed information, and how that information will be phrased.

The Media

Management must choose carefully the media used to disseminate news of venturing so employees will feel comfortable with the information they are receiving. When announcing a major change in corporate strategy, such as the development of a venturing program, it's better not to introduce flashy new public relations techniques. It is important to use media that the company's personnel are familiar with so they can concentrate on the message.

There are basically three types of media that should be used: people, written media, and production/communications media.

One person should serve as a central source of information. When several people are involved in disseminating information about a program, the information they give out must be timely and consistent from one person to the next. This is easier said than done when a number of executives must speak for the corporation to its employees, and when the new activity is not the executives' principal concern.

The company must give frequent updates so that all executives are regularly apprised of the situation. Although these executives don't need to be intimately involved in the day-by-day dissemination of information, employees must feel that their executives are knowledgeable, interested, and supportive of the program, or else they will see it as a failure before it starts. One way to take the load off of these executives would be to hold periodic company briefings, where employees could get the information they need all at once, either from the manager of their division or department, or from corporate representatives.

Most companies have an employee newspaper or newsletter. In addition to news of company picnics and softball game scores, this outlet can be used to explain the venturing program in detail and how it will affect the rest of the company. Employees should be encouraged to use the "Letters" column to maintain a continuing dialogue about their feelings and concerns.

Special pamphlets, brochures, posters, and other written media can be prepared, as well as videos, slide tapes, and other production media.

More companies every day are turning to computers as a medium for communicating company policy. Electronic bulletin boards are being used in companies that have extensive work-station networks. Systems such as the IBM-developed Professional Office System (PROFS) can be used to provide news of personnel changes, executive appointments, and reorganizations.

Many companies with these systems also have the capability for computer conferencing. Computer conferencing is a means of maintaining an ongoing dialogue on a number of subjects. Users can "subscribe" to any number of conference topics by getting the "key" into a particular file, and they can contribute their ideas to those of other conferees.

The Messenger

Regardless of how well the message is prepared, the diversity of media used, and the timeliness and frequency with which it is presented, there must be a real messenger. The messenger must carry the banner and demonstrate a sincere support for venturing.

Employees can easily discount electronic and printed messages as having been prepared by the employee-information or public-relations departments. At some point early in the process, employees need to hear management express its views directly. They need to ask questions and establish a dialogue with executives. At these sessions corporate executives and managers must convey their support of the new venture. They must also be able to explain the functional and structural organization of the venturing operation, as well as describe venturing management, background, skills, responsibilities, and activities.

The Venturing Image

The venturing image must be consistent with that of the corporation. Every successful company develops an image that employees take as part of themselves and that they support and enhance through their work. This is certainly the case with the IBMs of the world. There have been many cases of employees coming to work for IBM and not being particularly in the IBM mold at the outset. However, after enjoying the way they were perceived by the outside world as IBMers, they become part of the image, often unconsciously and often with the zeal only a convert can muster. When a company starts a new activity, it is crucial to employees that the company's image not be damaged.

Positive Career Impact

Management must also show that a venture, and the venturing business, is not a career dead end. Serving a tour of duty in a new organization must not be viewed as punishment. The company must show that a position in the new organization is an accepted part of the career path, that the assignment is professional according to corporate guidelines, and that it will contribute to individual advancement.

IBM did this successfully with one of its Independent Business Units (IBUs). The general manager of the unit was concerned that if employees looked at an assignment as the "end of their career," the IBU would only be able to obtain lower-quality employees, and that there would be minimal rotation in and out of the venturing, resulting in lower prospects for the venture's success. The general manager told his directors they must rotate people into other organizations in the company. This would ensure that the IBU would be continually revitalized with new skills and energy, employees' careers would be advanced, and the corporation would benefit from the exchange.

Ventures must be nurtured. The venture must be part of the organization that started it, yet able to function as a self-contained unit. Growth and success are possible only with the commitment of the total corporation. Material support can go only so far and has limited value without emotional commitment. Nourishment of ventures requires an environment that is hospitable, accepting, and encouraging.

Chapter Seven

Corporate Entrepreneurs: Finding Them and Harnessing Their Energy

Corporate entrepreneurs—often called intrapreneurs—are not the same as independent entrepreneurs. They have many of the same characteristics in terms of personality, relations with employers, and approaches to work, but there are fundamental differences.

The greatest of these differences can be seen in terms of their perception of risk and security, and their inclination to behave in ways that others perceive as risky. Corporate entrepreneurs are not willing to give up the security of a paycheck in order to begin their own business and test their own creativity and management. Because of this, they respond to various stimuli and risk/reward equations in ways very different from independent entrepreneurs.

Corporate entrepreneurs are unlike independent entrepreneurs in that they are less likely to have developed the broad range of skills necessary to run a business. They may not have dealt with budgets, supplies, and payrolls. They have probably not even thought about management trade-offs and basic issues of survival. A big issue for the independent entrepreneur may be the question of taking pay versus paying the employees.

Many corporate entrepreneurs have a low tolerance for management structure and bureaucracy. They are often technically oriented and primarily concerned with bending technology to their will. They are motivated and self-directed. When they have free time they turn to the "winners in the lower-left-hand-drawer." Most creative developers always have one or two such winners to work on.

For example, several years ago John, a bright MBA, was transferred to his company's business-analysis department after developing software for several years. He had always produced quality work, but he also annoyed managers because he set his own hours. On weekends, he could often be found in the office working on programs for handicapping horse races.

His new manager found that when John had a challenging assignment, he would come in early and leave late. On many occasions he worked through the night. He developed a number of innovative ideas. Although he continued to work on his race-handicapping programs, his performance was outstanding.

When his manager left on special assignment, the acting manager found this behavior intolerable. "I don't know what to do with him," the acting manager complained. Eventually, John left the company. Several years later, he became a vice-president for another large corporation that found his entrepreneurial orientation extremely valuable.

Corporate entrepreneurs have some traits in common with independent entrepreneurs, among them

- The ability to work amidst confusion
- The ability to anticipate change
- The ability to make intuitive leaps
- A high energy level and ability to concentrate
- Creativity in problem solving
- Action orientation

Corporate entrepreneurs are people who have ideas worth pursuing. They want not only to come up with the idea, but also to have intimate contact with it, and maybe even to have ultimate responsibility for carrying out the idea.

This is not the model that has been attributed to 3M and used by a number of other companies, where professional employees are able to use 10 or 15 percent of their company work time to be creative in the hope of developing products for the company. In many of these situations, the products are turned over to existing product-development operations.

Nor are we talking about the "entrepreneurial" manager, who is asked to try to run a company's division more like an entrepreneurial business, with less hierarchy and fewer layers of management.

WHO IS THE CORPORATE ENTREPRENEUR?

Corporate entrepreneurs are people who have, to varying degrees, the following characteristics:

1. They want a less restrictive work environment than they have experienced in the corporation.

2. They want to work on their own ideas, and they want those ideas to serve as a vehicle for advancement.
3. They want recognition for creativity.
4. They want recognition for marketing this creativity.
5. They are not willing to give up a regular paycheck.

The corporate entrepreneur is a person who has made some concessions in order to exist within the corporate structure. Those who have not made concessions have either left corporate life and are independent entrepreneurs, or they are corporate malcontents, a far different breed from the corporate entrepreneur. But this corporate entrepreneur is often at a stage where his or her career is stagnating because the entrepreneur either has not had visibility or is unwilling to make further concessions, especially the concessions necessary to go from more "line" or "hands-on" work to senior management.

The corporate entrepreneur is more likely not to be in management, but in the ranks of technical personnel. He or she might have reached the first level of line management, but may not be willing to adopt all of the company's policies and procedures necessary to become a senior manager.

Many corporate entrepreneurs turn their entrepreneurial talent to outside businesses while maintaining their jobs. One estimate is that about 10 percent of one large corporation's employees produce $500 million in revenue from such diverse businesses as cattle breeding, real estate development, auto rental agencies, auto repair, and personal services such as accounting, and a spectrum of retail businesses from picture framing to fast-food stands.

The corporate entrepreneur is outspoken without being abrasive. He or she is the person willing to open up and

tell the truth, even when it is not the most politically ex-
pedient thing to do. Corporate entrepreneurs come in all
sizes, shapes, colors, ages, and genders.

Many people dismiss older employees from consideration as possible corporate entrepreneurs. It's true that
some may be thinking of retirement, and others may have
had their ideas shot down so often that they are bitter and
have lost the creative spark. But many of these older employees are among the 10 percent of corporate employees
who have outside businesses. A good argument could be
made that the older employee would be the ideal corporate
entrepreneur, given the right person and the right conditions. The older employee has more experience and
more knowledge of the company. The older employee has
learned to roll with the corporate punches and is sensitive
to the parameters of corporate life. He or she understands
corporate sensitivities such as liability, exposure, and
image.

In short, the ideal corporate entrepreneur has internalized enough of corporate values to work within the system
to both his advantage and the company's, but at the same
time has not lost the entrepreneurial instinct.

REACHING OUT TO CORPORATE ENTREPRENEURS

A company looking to develop venturing must reach out to
those within the company who might be corporate entrepreneurs. There needs to be a public-relations effort that
explains how employees can get their ideas into the venturing loop. They must know what to do, how to present
ideas, and to whom.

The program must be visible. Those charged with finding these people and their ideas must go to operations sites and promote the idea that corporate entrepreneurship is acceptable and desirable. Managers must get the word from the front office that corporate entrepreneurship is a priority. They may need guidance in recognizing corporate entrepreneurs.

Once ideas and inquiries about the program start coming in, they must be responded to quickly. The person submitting an idea needs to know what is going to happen to the idea, what further input he or she should have, and when to expect some sort of an answer.

Corporate entrepreneurs must be assured of the confidentiality of their ideas. It must be explicitly stated that these people will retain "ownership" of the idea, that this is not an anonymous suggestion box. The reward comes when the idea is chosen, and the individual can be actively involved in putting it together as a working business. The entrepreneur may not become the manager of the new venture, but should at least be involved in follow-through.

CONCERNS IN DEALING WITH CORPORATE ENTREPRENEURS

There are four major concerns that companies should have when dealing with corporate entrepreneurs:

- They pay minimal attention to costs.
- They exaggerate potential and understate risks.
- They may have "entrepreneurial ego" issues, including a desire to retain independence for the project and a desire to retain personal control of the project.
- They may "overdevelop" projects both as a way to

maintain control and out of perfectionism, especially when working with one of their own ideas.

These concerns will be expanded on in the sections on funding, monitoring, and divesting of corporate ventures in later chapters. Suffice it to say that there may be conflicts between the desire to maintain good relations with a long-time employee and the need to manage a venture in a way that is best for the corporate investor.

COMPENSATING CORPORATE ENTREPRENEURS

The perception in many companies is that the penalties for failure outweigh the rewards for success. A good compensation plan should reverse that perception. To motivate potential entrepreneurs, compensation must be tailored to different levels of success.

Companies have always had problems compensating corporate innovators and entrepreneurs. One major problem stems from the practice of paying the principals in venture winners more than senior corporate executives. Another sensitive issue involves the question of rewarding corporate entrepreneurs without creating internal inequities and wreaking havoc with the company's overall compensation plan. This is one of Harold Geneen's reasons for doubting whether corporate entrepreneurship can work.

Corporate entrepreneurs deserve to be compensated in proportion to their contribution to the corporation. Any reward plan must be scaled to the level of risk and return. Considerations should include:

1. **The nature of the venture.** If the business or product is closely aligned with the corporation's mainline business,

there is obviously less risk than if the business is completely different. Consideration also must be given as to whether the venture will stand alone or depend on the company for a meaningful share of its support, and whether the business will be undertaken at the start-up, development, or research stage, each of which entails a different degree of risk.

2. **The nature of the expected return from the business.** The revenue obtained from the business should be separate from other revenue so that it can be measured. If not, the incremental income must be quantifiable so that the value of the idea can be determined.

3. **The entrepreneur's contribution and responsibilities.** Compensation must take into consideration that the entrepreneur may have two roles: as creator, inventor, and developer of the idea; and as a venture manager.

4. **Performance according to business case and original plan.** Measurement should consider slippage as well as budget overruns, and the reasons for either.

5. **The entrepreneur's risk.** In most cases the entrepreneur continues to draw full salary, with complete assurance that if the venture does not work out he or she still has a position with the company at full salary and benefits. Current thinking in some companies is that entrepreneurs should take a greater risk. Some people believe the corporate entrepreneur should give up salary increases while working with the venture until there are results that warrant additional compensation. In some cases, an entrepreneur may be asked to take a pay cut as a way of investing in the venture. In extreme cases, the entrepreneur loses his job with the company if the venture fails.

6. **How far the idea progressed through the new-business process.** Companies may want to reward employ-

ees for ideas advanced to the evaluation phase or beyond, even if they did not make it to a full-scale venture. This would encourage further participation by the employees rewarded and underscore the company's interest in receiving ideas and doing something with them.

7. **The time period over which any special compensation will be paid.** This is a critical issue because large sums of discretionary cash obtained through bonuses may actually encourage an entrepreneur to leave rather than stay to provide more ideas.

The company needs to make it clear from the beginning that the rewards for success are

- Based on the significance of the venture to the company's future
- A function of the company's risk and return
- Proportionate to the corporate entrepreneur's contribution
- Part of an overall corporate system. Since the company takes almost the entire risk in a corporate venturing effort, it simply cannot afford to offer the same kinds of rewards for winners that the open market does.

Many reward schemes focus on the amount of money that can be paid and ignore the fact that different entrepreneurs are driven by different objectives. Any compensation plan must have options that allow for the preferences of individual entrepreneurs. Some may want intangibles, such as more discretionary time to explore new ideas or more responsibility.

A plan should generally consist of four major categories of rewards: financial compensation, authority and responsibility, the freedom and resources to explore diverse interests, and general recognition. Any combination of these could be tailored to an entrepreneur's interests.

1. Financial rewards could include

- Salary increases
- Bonuses
- Corporate stock
- Creation of a new class of non-voting stock to be given to successful venture teams
- Perquisites such as vacation trips or scholarships for children's education

2. Authority and responsibility

- Promotions and projects to manage

3. New-idea exploration

- Time to explore new ideas
- Resources, such as support staff
- Funds for capital equipment and supplies

4. Recognition

- The possibilities include recognition in company publications, being honored at special events, and honorary positions.

The key to setting up a viable reward system for corporate entrepreneurs is to understand the culture of the company in which these people must operate, and the value system of the corporate entrepreneur. The specific reward schedule for any individual must meet with that person's agreement.

Finding and keeping corporate entrepreneurs is manageable and achievable. Failure to do this can only have a negative impact on venturing competitiveness and viability.

Chapter Eight

Organizational Options

The three models for setting up a successful corporate venture are

- The new-venture group
- The new-business unit
- The new-venture division

Although we do not advocate ad-hoc venturing, we can suggest some ways to improve the possibilities for success.

The new-venture group (NVG) is an in-house "venture-capital" type group that invests in internally created businesses. The NVG has the power of the purse, conducts all evaluations of potential ventures, and monitors all ventures during their lifetime, until they are ready to be transferred into the general fabric of the corporation as a separate business unit, operation, or division.

The new-business unit (NBU) is a department that acts as an advisory organization to working groups or task forces that are set up to develop and evaluate ideas for new businesses. These task forces might be ongoing or set up and disbanded as needed. The new-business unit is an in-house consulting group that uses its accumulated expertise in venturing to help task forces develop the skills needed for venturing, and to act as a clearinghouse for information on past venturing efforts.

The new-venture division (NVD) is a separate organization, with its own COO, within the corporation. It is similar to a new-venture group, except that the ventures become a part of the NVD.

Ad-hoc venturing is, unfortunately, the most common approach. It consists of establishing a venture whenever it seems like a good idea, the investment is affordable, and the company can make the necessary arrangements. Senior and line executives are directly involved in the funding, operation, and monitoring. These executives provide the principal ties to the corporation.

THE IDEAL AND THE REALITY

The new-venture group is the ideal. It most closely resembles an independent venture capital pool, giving those who work within it the flexibility to carry out the corporate venturing strategy with a minimum of interference. The most successful venturing will be that which is done as independently of the corporation as possible, away from the corporate behavior that rewards conservatism and punishes risk taking.

In a world with entirely rational behavior, we could envision a new-venture *division*. The division would function as an incubator for new ventures, providing administrative and other support to each venture. The venturing activity could be conducted in a more nurturing environment and in closer contact with the corporation than with a free-floating new-venture group. If the venture division were created from an already existing division that was entrepreneurially oriented, there would be an administrative infrastructure to draw on and an already established hierarchy and set of relationships with the corporate office.

Rarely, however, is there a corporate division that is entrepreneurially oriented. In one high-tech company, a division producing fairly pedestrian products got responsibility for several new products that were offbeat. With a stable business base, a corporate-style organization, and an entrepreneurially oriented chief executive, the division felt free to experiment with diverse products and markets and was quite successful. However, when the corporation decided to get more deeply into the venturing business, it went the ad-hoc route and lost the potential offered by this division.

The existing divisions of a corporation are usually ingrained in their current line of business and hinder ventures with their lack of entrepreneurial orientation and motivation. Although the division COO might be the right person to run a division full of new businesses, he or she may not be the right person to run a division that is also responsible for the process of finding, setting up, and determining the funding of those businesses.

THE CORPORATE LINK

Ventures set up within a corporation can benefit both the corporation and the venture entrepreneur. The corporation benefits by creating future potential and increasing the prospective net worth of the corporation with a relatively small investment. In turn, the venture has the protection of a large company, substantial resources to draw on, and support in many areas.

However, a venture also makes a company vulnerable. Venture activities could have an impact on the parent company's image, incur liability, and ultimately be a drain on company income. The corporate venture runs the risk of taking actions that could undermine company strategy. Some corporate ventures think of themselves as independent, or at least as something apart from the company, because of the preferential treatment they receive in some companies. Corporate management must ensure that venture executives always keep in mind that they are part of a larger organization.

Guidelines must be set that:

1. Identify powers reserved to corporate management.
2. Identify the corporate policies and directives that are applicable to ventures.
3. Clarify the product areas in which the venture will be involved.

THE NEW-VENTURE GROUP

In the real world, the most desirable structure for a venturing organization within a corporation is the quasi-independent new-venture group. This group, comprised of from two to five principals (depending on the scope of venturing and the size of the fund to be managed) and minimal support staff, is a self-contained group, analogous to an independent venture capital fund.

The money to fund both the group and the investments it will make will be made available, either in a lump sum payment at the beginning of the group's tenure, or in annual installments for the first few years of the group's life. Salaries and other incentives for group members will come out of this fund and should equal about 2 to 3 percent of the total fund annually. This is analogous to the independent venture capitalist's management fee. We will discuss the fee further in Chapter 10.

Responsibilities

In this model, the new-venture group has a fiduciary responsibility to the corporation, as an independent venture capital fund has to its investors, and will report to the corporation (usually directly to the CEO) as often as needed for management's peace of mind, probably quarterly.

This venture group is responsible for all phases of venturing activity, and the focus of its work will change over time. If the NVG is investing a fixed amount, the total "life" of the unit will probably be somewhere between 10 and 15 years. Evidence from independent venture capitalists shows that it takes about five years for the fund to become fully invested, and seven to 10 years for all of the ventures to reach the stage of maturity when the new-venture group can turn them over to corporate management to be run as "adolescent" businesses within the corporation in general.

In the first phase of activity, which will usually last several months, the new-venture group is responsible for developing awareness within the company of the venture group, creating a process for collecting ideas, giving feedback on ideas, and developing the proper reward system for those who generate ideas. The group will have to publicize the process and the idea of venturing in general.

As ideas begin to flow, the main task of the group begins—to evaluate the potential ventures, and to find the ones that fit the company's strategy and criteria and have the potential to be successful businesses. The group is also developing a data base, not only of the specific ideas that worked or didn't work, but also of the evaluative methods they used. They might coach would-be entrepreneurs about how to get their ideas into a presentable form for review, and how to structure the process of sorting, screening, and evaluating.

Working with Venture Management

Once ventures begin to be put together, the new-venture group must divide its time between working with the ventures and looking for more good ideas to invest in. The group must negotiate with the management team of each venture about funding, milestones, measurements, and monitoring techniques. The entrepreneur and investor must agree to certain conditions. This is different from the corporation or manager giving an employee a plan to follow.

Most venture capitalists say that in this phase of operations, when there are ongoing ventures and the need to invest in more, they are spending anywhere from 30 to 60 percent of their time actively managing and/or monitoring their investments. The NVG will need to meet weekly to make sure that investments, as well as current evaluations, are progressing smoothly.

Transfer Activities

After a number of years, probably not until after the venture group is fully funded, there will come a time to cash out of, or divest, the ventures. In the world of independent venture capitalists, this cashing out is done either by the company's going public, with the venture capitalists selling off most or all of their stock in the initial public offering, or by the company's being sold to a larger, publicly traded company, and the venture capitalists' getting either cash or stock in the purchasing company.

The corporate analog to this takes the form of turning the venture over to the corporate parent, to continue either as a separate operating unit or to become a part of an ongoing division.

There is much anecdotal evidence to show that many companies lose their entrepreneurial tenor when they become part of a larger company. There is a stage of corporate growth—business adolescence—that calls for a style of management that is not as entrepreneurial as in start-up companies but that is not as formal as in mature companies. Venture capitalists have long known that by the time a venture reaches about $15 million in sales, new management is usually needed to take the venture through the adolescent phase. Even when entrepreneurs have previously agreed to step down at this stage, they often resist, forcing venture capitalists to use their power as major investors and their membership on the venture company's board to bring in a new management team.

The new-venture group may be asked as part of its task to set up a management structure for a venture before it turns the business over to the corporation. If this is part of the venture group's task, the NVG ought to give thought early in the venture's lifetime to creating a structure for the orderly integration of the ventures into the corporate structure, dealing with such issues as how it will make the management transition, how long before it envisions cashing out, and what will happen to the ventures that have not reached that point when the life of the venture group runs out.

THE NEW-BUSINESS UNIT

The new-business unit model sets up a group—about the same size as the new-venture group—that acts essentially as the staff to the decision makers who will create new businesses.

Currently, many companies use task forces to conduct all kinds of business, including the development of both internal and external ventures. The new-business unit has as one of its main virtues that it fits very well with a task-force model of corporate activity. The NBU becomes the permanent staff to a variety of task forces that are set up intermittently, do their job, and are then disbanded. The NBU can be thought of in similar terms to the permanent civil-service undersecretary in a parliamentary government—the cabinet minister changes, but the undersecretary stays the same. (Figure 8-1)

In this model, the NBU serves two main functions:

1. To support management in efficient and effective development of new businesses by helping to select the best opportunities and implementing the strategy of the venturing plan. To do this, the NBU assists task forces to go "up the learning curve" of venturing more quickly than if the task force had to learn by itself, and to do much of the staff work in the venture decision-making process.

2. To provide continuity and consistency in receiving and processing all ideas and then following through in supporting the evaluation, establishment of the venture, and continued monitoring. The NBU does this primarily by

Figure 8-1. NBU Role in Venturing Process

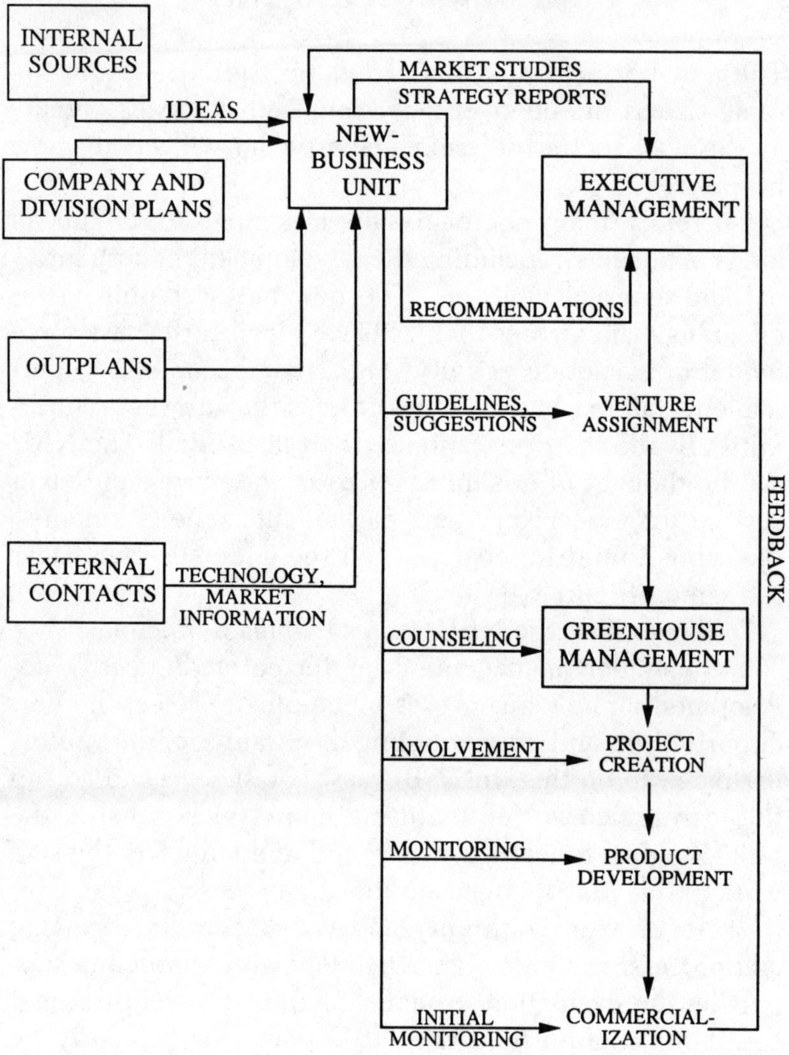

being a repository for the corporation's data base with regard to venturing, both in terms of the techniques of venturing and in terms of the company's prior venturing activity. Rather than allowing the records of any task force on venturing to be discarded or put into "dead storage" after the task force is disbanded, the NBU would preserve and use those records.

One of the reasons an NBU can be so helpful to task forces is that, in the business world, the task force concept has become overused and misused. Task forces have become study-and-recommendation groups, rather than problem-solving and action teams, which they were originally designed to be.

Task-Force Problems

The task force is an outgrowth of the operations-analysis concept first developed in World War II. The idea was to get a number of people with different kinds of expertise and apply their talents to solving a particular problem. People with different backgrounds would see problems from different angles, and as a group they could explore creative solutions.

Over the years, however, this understanding and optimal use of the corporate task force has been lost. Executives and managers who are already very busy are loath to sit in groups trying to solve problems. Management has also forgotten the requirement that highly capable people are needed for effective task forces. Because of this, task forces are often composed of people who are available, not very critical to company operations, not very creative, and expendable to their managers ("I can let so-and-so go for a month").

If one person with these qualities is on a task force, he or she can slow it down, the chain being only as strong as its weakest link. Managers of executives who want to stifle or sabotage certain plans need only to appoint task force members who will not work effectively with other members. When task forces are loaded with these people, little gets done, and it is difficult to get senior executives to "buy into" the solutions developed by the task force; if these people were task force material, how good can their solutions be, anyway?

In addition, task forces often become large and unwieldy. In order not to antagonize a particular constituency, someone representing that group may be allowed to participate in the task force, despite the fact that the larger the decision-making body, the longer the process takes, and the harder it is to come to any real decisions.

Despite what we have said about the new-venture group's being our ideal, in the corporate reality where control is such a big issue, the new-business unit is more likely to be implemented. Because of this, we'd like to explore this idea in detail. This is a generic plan that can be tailored to any particular company.

NBU Tasks

The NBU would first be responsible for designing the mechanisms of venturing. These fall in four general areas and present the NBU with its first tasks:

1. To develop materials for both idea advocates—those who propose ideas to the venture decision makers—and the task forces that will decide on ventures. Idea advocates need to understand the requirements for proposals, as well as management's criteria for evaluation and ultimate selec-

tion. At the same time, task forces must be provided with techniques, criteria, and operating information that will help them understand the nature of venturing.

2. To develop material regarding the makeup of ventures, so task forces know exactly what they will be creating. Areas to be defined include key success factors, needed skills, and the desired organizational climate.

3. To develop a general approach for the interaction between ventures and the parent company, and the points of interface between the two entities. These areas include the level of site services and the level and source of staff support in areas such as business practices, design automation, manufacturing sources, personnel programs, pricing, communications, and contracts, both with consultants and with customers.

4. To create the new-venture data base. The NBU would need to establish and maintain a historical file of evaluations, decision criteria, project progress, and actions taken with regard to ventures.

In addition, the NBU would be responsible for training each task force before it begins looking into proposals. Task forces usually increase the cost of new-business evaluations because there is minimal data and little accumulation of experience from prior evaluations. If other task forces are set up to monitor ventures, the NBU would also train those task forces. However, the monitoring function could be more efficiently accomplished by the NBU itself, which could provide at least some level of continuity because of its involvement in the evaluation process.

Many other tasks may be assigned to the NBU at management's discretion. The NBU may be charged with stimulating employee interest in developing and submitting ideas, or at least being the central receiving point for all new business proposals. In this case, the NBU could have a sorting role and recommend ideas to the evaluation task force.

The NBU would also have intermediary functions, such as deciding where a venture should be positioned organizationally and geographically. Placement, as this is called, followed by creating the project team, and monitoring, all require interaction with all levels of executive staff and line personnel on technical, administrative, and operational matters. In placement, the NBU would work with corporate staffs, with personnel from divisions selected as greenhouse sites, and with the executives responsible for the venture.

Supporting the Venture

With regard to each individual venture, the NBU would have three main functions (Figure 8-2):

1. Supporting the establishment of the venture by helping to create the management team—one of the most critical factors in establishing a venture—and being the liaison between the venture and the operating unit in which it will be situated.

2. Working with the venture management in planning, tracking performance, troubleshooting, and providing contacts and access to resources within the corporation.

3. Supporting the corporation's risk-management function, including ongoing monitoring of the venture. The NBU would also establish and review milestone development plans, assist management in assessing project risks, and create a plan for transfer of the venture into the main-

Figure 8-2. New-Business Unit Responsibilities

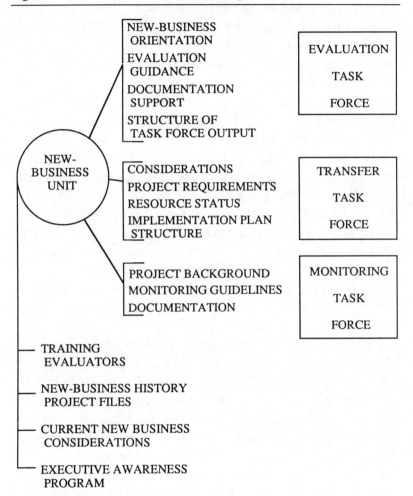

NEW-BUSINESS
  ORIENTATION
EVALUATION
  GUIDANCE
DOCUMENTATION
  SUPPORT
STRUCTURE OF
  TASK FORCE OUTPUT

EVALUATION

TASK

FORCE

NEW-
BUSINESS
UNIT

CONSIDERATIONS
PROJECT REQUIREMENTS
RESOURCE STATUS
IMPLEMENTATION PLAN
  STRUCTURE

TRANSFER

TASK

FORCE

PROJECT BACKGROUND
MONITORING GUIDELINES
DOCUMENTATION

MONITORING

TASK

FORCE

TRAINING
  EVALUATORS

NEW-BUSINESS HISTORY
  PROJECT FILES

CURRENT NEW BUSINESS
  CONSIDERATIONS

EXECUTIVE AWARENESS
  PROGRAM

line business or sale to an outside party for each venture as early in the venture's life as possible.

The NBU's functions in many ways parallel those of the new-venture group, except that the NBU does not have the funding authority, and so acts in more of a staff capacity for those who make funding decisions. The NBU would be more directly beholden to corporate management, and would have less flexibility in its venture-advocacy role than would a venture group. The NBU would have a different breakdown of how much of its time is spent in various functions than the venture group would, since it has many more direct contacts with management.

In addition, corporate management may give the NBU the added task of working with executives to keep current its new-business policy statements, strategies, and program plans; and further supporting the venture task forces, entrepreneurs, venture management teams, and corporate executives who oversee new business by providing them with reports on business trends.

The NBU must interact well on all corporate levels. It should have high standing by reporting to one of the corporation's top four or five officers. Ideally, there should be an advisory board, of which this executive is part, that decides on funding and exercises management prerogatives on behalf of the corporation. This responsibility and authority require that the board be knowledgeable and involved with the NBU's venturing activities. The frequency of board oversight on the NBU would probably be less than that of the new-venture group because the NBU has no funding authority.

Additionally, the NBU would maintain extensive contacts outside the company, with both venture capital organizations and other companies engaged in new-business development, in order to keep up with the latest trends, technologies, markets, industries, and venturing techniques.

NEW-VENTURE DIVISION

As has been said, in an ideal world the new-venture division would be the best solution, but because of corporate realities it is probably the least suitable solution. If the corporation is willing to let the venture division operate autonomously, it can work, but the corporation must make an ironclad commitment not to interfere with the venture division. The division COO should not be put in the position of having to sacrifice the goals of venturing for the sake of short-term considerations.

An existing division should be considered as a candidate for the new-venture division only if

1. It can take on the new venture mission with a minimum of disruption.
2. Venturing is highly compatible with the division's organization.
3. It can begin its venturing activities with minimal delay.

The division that is chosen to be the venture division must have the qualities, infrastructure, and support one would find in a stand-alone company. It should be an integrated operation, with its own administrative and financial structure.

It should have the proper organizational climate, and a

philosophy and psychology in which people are comfortable working in a "cats-and-dogs" environment, almost as a "job shop," in that people do a number of tasks on a variety of particular jobs in any one day.

In a corporate division one must expect some compartmentalization. But in a new-venture division there must be a high level of interaction, and people must be willing and able to work in small groups. The division should be business-oriented, rather than R&D-oriented. Even the administration and support-function staff must be comfortable working with a number of diverse business situations and problems. As soon as possible the division must transfer out all businesses that are not part of the venturing effort. All resources must be devoted to the growing group of new businesses.

Organizationally, there should be a small new-venture group within the new-venture division that puts together a new-idea program (which can also draw ideas from outside the division), as well as handling all the evaluations. Whether the small NVG can invest funds, or whether it makes recommendations to the divisional COO, is a matter of choice.

Venture divisions fail for a number of reasons.

When they are established using ongoing divisions, the wrong type of division is usually chosen. The division's mindset is often too compartmentalized, and its orientation and activities are usually geared toward running fewer and larger established business entities.

When venture divisions are established from scratch, problems derive from key personnel not having worked together previously. They may require a break-in period of anywhere from one to three years in order to feel comfortable with one another. They may not be used to working with small businesses. These problems exist in addition to those relating to the organization, staffing, facilities, and other tasks involved in starting a new operation.

AD-HOC VENTURING

With this approach the cards are stacked against both the venture and the company. Some things can be done to reduce the probability of failure without forcing the company to pigeonhole its venturing effort into one of our models.

One company came to that conclusion in a very logical way. During the late 1970s, the company began laying the groundwork for a series of new ventures. In 1980 the company announced several venturing efforts. A year later the company issued a corporate management memorandum that described this type of organization, how it would operate and, as one of the attachments, guidelines that addressed the applicability of, or exceptions to, existing or new corporate policies, practices, procedures, and programs.

Three years later a revision of the corporate management memo sought to clarify the new-venture concept and "increase management control" of them. In an explanatory note, the memo stated that the "intent of the actions taken is best summarized as the desire to tighten responsibility for plan and performance evaluation . . . but not impose unnecessary restrictions or overly manage or control new business opportunities. This includes a more carefully thought through strategy and understanding of the proposal prior to applying" the new-venture concept.

What the company found was not ventures that had gone out of control, but a venturing system that, because it had no guidelines, could not impose the control necessary to channel entrepreneurship into successful businesses.

The memo spoke of "the need for greater basic business controls . . . including administrative plan and control methods and procedures." The directive to corporate executives involved with these ventures was to "initiate new actions required, such as establishing checkpoints" for each new venture.

To do this, a company must take the same steps that the organizations established in the three formal options would have to do:

1. Define the areas in which a venture would be bound by corporate guidelines, policies, practices, procedures, and programs.

2. Establish guidelines for evaluating and selecting prospective ventures. Since different groups may be doing the evaluations and different executives will be making the decisions and become involved with the ventures, consistency is needed.

After substantial investment and personal hardship by some venture personnel, a company would like to avoid the type of comment made by the executive of one new corporate venture: "We concluded that, even though we were successful . . . it was inconsistent" with the company's objectives.

3. Document the results of all evaluations and decisions as a reference for future discussions and monitoring of the venture.

4. Establish a group of "venture directors" to meet to consult on start-up problems and to support the venture management.

5. Agree on a business plan and establish milestones that

will be monitored, with continued funding dependent on milestone achievement.

The bottom line is that whatever a corporation calls its new-venture organization, it must think through the variables and set up mechanisms for orderly evaluation and management control before it begins establishing ventures.

Chapter Nine

Staffing the Internal Venturing Group

Venture capital firms almost invariably consist of a small group of principals, with little or no staff. The principals do their own research and evaluative work and, working alone or in small teams, are able to make quick decisions.

Using the same model for the corporate-venturing function concentrates the decision making and avoids overstaffing. The new-venture group should consist of from three to five principals, depending on the size of the fund to be administered. The group could start with three members, and as it progresses into funding a number of projects and needing to monitor them, one or two positions are added. One to three staff people should be enough for even the largest fund.

The new-business unit, or its analog within a new-venture division, would need as many principals as the new-venture group. The new-business unit has a different scope of work from that of the new-venture group, but one that is as intense and detail-oriented, assuming the same level of overall venturing activity.

Generally, corporate venture-capital operations have

both more principals and larger support staffs than independent venture-capital firms. Companies usually have support-staff people do most of the research work on prospective ventures. Because corporations do not compensate either principals or staff people as well as the independent firms would if they were principals, many of the best people leave to start their own firms or join established venture-capital groups. As a result, many companies "double-staff" to provide for turnover.

Nevertheless, corporations must keep these venture-business groups small, and deal with the problem of turnover by making new-venture management a part of the executive career path. Since this group will be critical to the company's future, management must negotiate with those who become involved in the venture activity about the term of their assignment, and they must create a compensation and incentive package that is attractive.

All too often the corporate-venturing function is considered off the managerial or executive growth track, and people become anxious at being off that track for too long. In other companies, a tour with a venturing activity is considered good training, and only "fast-track" people get a chance.

When a company takes the right approach to and is committed to venturing, people who join the venture activity will be more receptive and more likely to make a career commitment to it. But at the minimum, these people should be prepared to stay for five years, and the company should plan on this. In the "fast-track" scenario, future executives can be expected to move on in about two years, before they really know what is going on and can be expected to have any major impact on the new-venture business.

One way to start the venture business is to bring in a

principal from the independent venture-capital world. This will be very difficult to do; not only must the compensation and incentive package be attractive, but the person must be willing and able to work within the corporate milieu, and not easily frustrated by corporate bureaucracy.

PROFILE OF A VENTURIST

In the past, few venture capitalists had legal or technical backgrounds. Many more had backgrounds in money management. Several venture capitalists interviewed for an earlier study said they thought that a stronger technical background would be helpful but not absolutely necessary. Today more venture capitalists have technical training.

Personability, good negotiating skills, and the willingness to do group brainstorming and problem solving are also qualities high on the list. The "chemistry" between entrepreneurs and venturists is critical to creating a good basis for working together closely. Many of the most successful venture capitalists come across as firm, yet sensitive, individuals, and they seem to be imbued with a personal warmth that suggests that assistance would always be available to the entrepreneur when needed.

Good venturists are quick learners and must be able to size up imprecise situations. They must be able to sort out the important facts and critical areas of importance from the "boilerplate" presented by entrepreneurs, or the mountains of unnecessary information provided by technical geniuses with no sense of presentation values.

Honesty and integrity would seem to be givens; however, in interviews most venture capitalists voiced these qualities as essential to themselves and people they would work with. Flexibility, independence of attitude, the willingness and ability to articulate one's reasoning, and an enjoyment of the process are seen by most venture capitalists as critical to long-term success. Stan Golder, former president of the National Venture Capital Association, said in an interview that the key characteristic for a successful venturist is "a super ego, with the right combination of self-confidence and self-doubt." The internal corporate venturist should have these qualities, and be able to use them within the confines of the operational guidelines one would find in a corporate situation.

If the venturing function is constituted as a new-business unit or a new-business division, these people will also have to be willing to accept their role as an advisor, sublimate their egos, and allow others to make the final decisions— one of the weaknesses of the NBU concept.

In the new-business unit set-up, the principals must blend the inherently entrepreneurial characteristics of the independent venture capitalists with the characteristics of the good staff person. They must be willing and able to take on the training function inherent in being a permanent in-house consulting unit that helps newly appointed task forces get up to speed on venturing.

A company may find it helpful to get assistance from an independent venture capitalist in "hiring" the staff for the newly created corporate venture group. The tendency is to hire people with like outlooks, and corporate executives might not be the best people to hire for an internal venture function.

POTENTIAL AND PERFORMANCE

Assessing the potential and performance of venturing personnel is difficult. As one venture capitalist said, "You can't find experienced people in this business. You look for certain kinds of experience and abilities and develop the other skills."

The key in the venture-capital industry for measuring newly hired associates is their ability to build up the partners' confidence in their judgment. Many of the same qualities are sought in internal venturists. Prospective venture-group employees would be evaluated based on such factors as

- Their approach to deals
- How they handle entrepreneurs
- How good they are at rewriting business plans
- How they negotiate
- How good the investments are that they bring in
- Their ability to convince others of the quality of an investment
- How many investments they have generated
- Their relationships with venture capitalists, entrepreneurs, members of the venture-group and possibly with people in the industry
- How much responsibility they take
- Their understanding of how a business works
- Their ability to identify the "real problem" in any given situation
- Their demonstration of good insight

Evaluating performance is equally difficult, one venture capitalist says, because a new venture capitalist "is not really effective before two years." Depending on the way the venturing function is constituted within a corporation, some or all of the qualities venture capitalists judge as valuable should also be sought in potential internal venturists. Regardless of the organizational structure of the internal venturing body, good analytical skills and good "people" skills should be considered paramount.

Chapter Ten

Funding

When a company says it is making a commitment to venturing, it should put its money where its mouth is. Funding is the glue that holds the venturing operation together. The funding level cannot be vulnerable, it cannot be dependent on the level of sales, profits, or R&D expenditures. The venturing team must know that it has the financial wherewithal to make long-term commitments. Corporations tend to fund venturing the same way they fund R&D. In fact, a number of business observers have said R&D and venturing serve the same purpose.

Funding levels for venturing and R&D are often set as a percentage of sales. This policy is contrary to the company's best interests. As sales decline—either due to market or business conditions or due to obsolescence of the company's products—R&D and venturing also begin to decline, just when expenditures in these areas should be increasing in order for the company to regain its market share. When the company is doing well, management thinks it can gamble on ventures or R&D, but when it is not doing well, management becomes cautious.

There are psychological reasons for this. When things are going well, corporate managements are likely to have a positive attitude about business and the prospects for development of new businesses. R&D and venture funding tend to move in one direction for a number of years, until the general consensus is that it has gone too far. This pendulum effect creates a number of problems, such as staff cutbacks, forcing a choice among a number of in-progress projects, and an inability to plan long-term.

BREAKING THE CYCLE

Companies must break this traditional pattern of funding when it comes to the corporate venturing effort. This means funding the new-venture operation consistent with corporate diversification objectives and strategy. By definition it must be supported to the extent necessary to allow it to function smoothly. It is better to fund fewer projects than to fail to nurture each ongoing project with the necessary amount of money.

There is a fundamental difference between R&D and venturing. R&D is a continuing effort that produces sporadic results. New developments, when successfully transferred into product-oriented divisions, follow a fairly well-defined path to product status and market. Rarely do these developments become the basis for a separate organization, as with venturing.

Unlike R&D, an internal venturing effort can adhere to a plan. Although ideas for ventures may not arrive on a timetable, management can have some assurance that within a designated period they will find good candidates to fund.

Managing the Costs

Venturing is proportionately more expensive than R&D. Setting up a new organization to house the venture entails organization costs. Support functions that enable a business to stand alone are also necessary, even though they may duplicate those elsewhere in the corporation.

The overhead costs of successful venturing are also greater than in R&D. The lowest costs of management and administration are obtained with the new-venture group structure. The new-business unit will probably have lower known costs for the same level of effort, but the costs of task forces, losses due to personnel reassignments, and executive time will boost the total expense beyond that of the new-venture group. The costs of a new-venture division are variable, because each company will have its own organizational style. With this option the company is also more likely to include the cost of space, furniture, and fixtures, such as word processors and copying machines, in the financial analysis of the new-venture business. Companies differ widely in valuing the costs of accounting, legal, and other services. The independent start-up uses and pays for these services on an as-needed basis, usually by the hour.

Corporations are concerned with exposure as well as expenditures. At IBM, most IBUs have their own financial support, legal counsel, and, in most situations, a business-practices person. This increases the cost of the venture but lowers the exposure.

Ad-hoc venturing costs the most when all costs are accumulated and the failure rate is taken into account. In the unstructured new-business environment of most companies, these random, usually fruitless, efforts are not accounted for, but they involve real costs in the form of time lost on current assignments while personnel are making the rounds of executive contacts, developing and delivering presentations, and preparing material requested by executives.

FUNDING APPROACHES FOR THE VENTURE OPERATION

There are three ways to fund the venture operation:

- An investment pool
- Annual payments
- A case-by-case arrangement

The first two ways assume that the organization is either a new-venture group or a new-venture division. The third option assumes that the organizational structure is that of a new-business unit. But however the money flows to the venturing team, and ultimately to the ventures funded, it must be set aside in the corporate budget as a line item for each of a specified number of years.

Option 1: The Venture-Capital Fund

This is the option that most closely mimics the set-up used by independent venture capitalists. It is also the option that allows the venturing team the most flexibility, and therefore is the ideal set-up for the new-venture group structure.

In this set-up, the new-venture group (or new-venture division) gets a "pot" of money at the beginning of its tenure and is told to come back after the term of the program—eight, 10, or maybe 15 years later—having achieved its objectives. A percentage return on investment is likely to be one of the venture group's goals.

In the world of independent venture capitalists, a prospectus is published that tells potential investors the rules of the game—the minimum investment, the hoped-for results, the investment strategy and guidelines, the life of the fund, the risk, and a host of other variables. In the corporate model the corporation is the fund's sole investor, and sets the rules for the venture team managing the fund.

Venture-capital firms use "rounds" of funding to indicate when investment is required beyond that originally provided for. The equivalent condition exists in the corporation, in the continuing need for more funds. Each year there is a review, and often the scope of work and financial data must be modified. Reasons for increases in funding include slippage in achieving milestones, expansion in the scope of work, and redirection of the effort.

The venture-capitalist philosophy—essentially "project-life-cycle" or "program" costing—must be used by companies in their venturing efforts. Developed by Charles Hitch of the RAND Corporation in the 1950s, life-cycle costing was adopted by Secretary of Defense Robert McNamara in 1961 and successfully used in managing the growing inventory of weapon systems in development. In the mid-1960s, this approach was used in an IBM division for planning, evaluating, and selecting all R&D projects.

Assuming that progress-based funding will be provided when particular milestones are reached, funds would have to be held in reserve through the eighth or ninth year for later-phase financing of projects that are funded in the fourth or fifth years of a venture program.

Funds in the investment pool must remain separate from

venture proceeds. By the ninth or tenth year, ventures funded in the early years may be showing positive cash flow and possibly even an overall profit. Even if these ventures remain separate and have not been integrated into an existing business operation, their income must not be used for other investments. Any commingling of funds creates problems in accountability and determining the return of investments, and undermines the corporation's agreement with the venturing activity.

We may assume that successful ventures will be "divested" by incorporating them into the parent corporation as an "adolescent," or ongoing, business. Companies have different objectives from those of venture capitalists, and are not looking for financial return from selling off ventures that have succeeded financially.

Poor or failing ventures will be discontinued, with the assets, technology, or the entire operation sold to someone outside the company, or the technology will be integrated into the technology base of a related ongoing business unit.

One large corporation sold two product lines from an unsuccessful venture to two different companies. In one sale, both the technology and product were sold. In the other sale, the basic technology was sold without the test results, with the condition that the purchaser would have to revalidate the results before building products around it.

Any cash received for ventures sold usually offsets only part of the loss, because the sale agreement usually contains the condition that the purchaser will service existing customers. The key advantage for corporations is that they have fulfilled their responsibility and kept faith with existing customers.

One should not hope to put up a small amount at the

beginning, and parlay profits from one venturing success into other ventures.

Option 2: The Five-Year Plan

This is really a variation on Option 1, used by companies that want to control the amount invested annually as well as in total. In this option, the venture kitty would be paid in equal installments to the venturing team over a number of years—usually about five. The annual amount may go uncommitted in some years, and may constrain funding worthwhile ventures in future years unless funds can be carried forward on the books.

This must not be a "use-it-or-lose-it" budget, where the level of funding in one year depends on the level of spending from the previous year. Funding will be necessary for three to five years after the corporation has finished paying out the pool to the venturing operation; therefore, the venture team must be able to bank portions of each year's corporate contribution.

Fund management may be more difficult under this arrangement. However, corporate financial types will readily adopt this system because it conforms to the annual planning cycles. The semiannual plans, or the twice-a-year planning cycles, one for the near term and the other for the overall strategic planning period, will provide the financial community with the data for cash flows, expected expenditures, contingencies, and other projections.

Using the five-year example, a $15 million fund would be paid in increments of $3 million per year. This option is better suited to the new-venture division, since divisions are often funded on an annual basis. Although a venturing division may be expected to continue indefinitely, investment periods should be defined as a basis for measurement.

While the annual-payments alternative is a more difficult way to fund, it can work. However, it needs to be clear from the beginning that this funding cannot and will not be turned off. If this is merely a mechanism for company management to rethink venturing each year, the program is doomed to failure before it gets started.

Option 3: The Business Case-by-Case Fund

This, in essence, is the only option for the new-business unit organizational structure or the ad-hoc approach. The NBU, acting as a clearinghouse and a group of internal consultants, will help task forces make recommendations to whatever corporate entity is making final decisions about venture funding. Then, while the NBU is conducting monitoring and oversight, others will have to worry about the money.

Case-by-case funding provides the easiest opportunity for the corporation to back out of its commitment to venturing, since there is really no independent venturing group that has a say in funding and that can act as an advocate for individual ventures and the venturing process in general.

No matter what funding option is chosen, funding coverage must be tied to the scope of work. A key question to answer is, will the venturing team be allowed to fund only proposals selected for development, or will the group be allowed to "buy the time" of people who have ideas that need more thought and work before they can be presented in a coherent business plan?

In addition, the new-venture business may have to contract for technical consultants to help either in the preparation of a business plan or in the review of a business plan for a potential venture.

On occasion, venture capitalists work with entrepreneurs to refine their business plans and will hire consultants to aid in evaluating a plan. There is also precedent for corporations not asking corporate entrepreneurs to use all their own time—3M being probably the best example. And entrepreneurs will often say they have "liberated" time, services, and other things from their legitimate employers in an effort to develop an idea to the business-plan stage.

COST OF THE VENTURING STAFF

Unfortunately, companies have the tendency to add people, invoking the principle of "more is better," if a project is in difficulty, or if there is some uncertainty about what to do.

One way of containing the number of people is to use the venture-capitalist model, where the cost of staffing the corporate venture function is the equivalent of the venture capitalist's management fee, which is a percentage of the total investment pool. For our hypothetical $15 million venture pool, the staffing and budget should cost between 2.25 and 3 percent, roughly $325,000 to $450,000, per year, averaged over the life of the fund.

A phased approach is best, with additional staff being taken on in Year Two or Year Three of the venturing function, as the workload increases. Some allowance may be made for bringing people on earlier than needed depend-

Table 10-1   Hypothetical Budget for Three Years

	1st year	2nd year	3rd year
Staffing:			
Principals	2	4	4
Support	1–2	2	2
Budget ($000)			
Salaries	$240	$430	$450
Travel	20	30	35
Miscellaneous (publications, conferences, education)	5	10	15
TOTAL	$265	$470	$500
Percentage of fund	1.7	3.0	3.3
	2.7 percent average		

ing on their experience and the amount of training that will be required (Table 10-1).

At this point, inflation and cost-of-living increases will account for budget increases each year. (This does not take into account other incentives that may have been set up, and performance-based compensation.)

These figures assume a director of the venture function with a base salary of about $125,000, and principals being paid about $85,000 each.

The budget and salaries assume a return to the principals on successful ventures, which for most venture capital firms is about 20%.

FUNDING VENTURES

Years ago, in the course of developing an annual eight-figure R&D program for an advanced-technology division of IBM, 300 requests from researchers were evaluated annually. Despite all the economic analysis that had been done by staff, the bottom-line question remained to be asked of each individual researcher: "Assuming you were asked, would you put up 1 percent of your budget request out of your own pocket?" We looked for one thing: how fast the researcher said yes.

Venture capitalists expect significant financial commitments from entrepreneurs (significant in respect to what the entrepreneur actually has). In the corporate setting, financial commitment by entrepreneurs is only hypothetical, but the answer to "Would you commit?" is still valuable to the venture group.

The guidelines for managing a corporate venture fund are by and large the same as for an independent fund:

- Take a portfolio approach.
- Fund upon achievement of specific milestones.
- Invest about two-thirds of the fund, and save about one-third for contingencies.
- Try to be fully invested in about five years.

Portfolio Approach

A portfolio approach means using the company's investment criteria to put together a balanced group of ventures. A few tips about portfolios:

- There should be different levels of investment, some large and some small.
- Ventures should take different amounts of time to get to market. For example, not all ventures should be in the development stage.
- Ventures should depend on different technologies. Not every venture should need breakthroughs to be state-

of-the-art, and not all should have the same technology as their base.

- Ventures should depend on complementary competencies. Not all ventures should be market-driven or technology-driven. Some should be product-oriented, some service-oriented.

By diversifying ventures, results can be measured at different times throughout the life of the fund. Corporate management often feels a need to show results fast, and a venture needs to pan out quickly to get continued funding. But the rules of venturing don't follow these corporate laws. Good ideas—especially for products or services at the development stage—don't always come to the attention of the venture group early in the process.

Proper development of a balanced portfolio can take place only in an atmosphere where the company has made an ironclad commitment to long-term funding.

Milestone Funding

Despite the corporate-funding model based on annual budgeting, individual ventures need to be funded on a milestone basis. The development of realistic yet aggressive milestones at the beginning of a venture provides the venture group with an easy way to monitor a venture's activities. The venture is forced to think ahead of time about its real needs, and to put the progress it hopes to make toward a goal into an incremental framework.

Two-thirds Investment, One-third Contingency

Because it is often difficult to gauge the true cost of a venture at its beginning, especially if it deals with technology that will need breakthroughs, it is important for corporate venture groups to maintain adequate contingency funding. This is compounded by the fact that entrepreneurs are notorious for underestimating the true cost of their activities.

Most venture capitalists use a two-thirds investment, one-third contingency rule, and even though their thinking in this regard may differ from that of corporate venturists, it is not a bad rule to stick by. Venture capitalists, even if they know that it will take 150 to 200 percent of the estimated budget to actually fund the venture, may allow the entrepreneur to underestimate at the beginning, and fund the venture at the level projected, for a couple of reasons. One is that when the entrepreneur comes back for more funding, the venture capitalist may be able to exert more influence over the company's management by pointing out how fast the money went. The other is that by additional funding later, the venture capitalists can acquire greater control. Rather than negotiating harder at the beginning, getting the entrepreneur to take more money (which the venture capitalist knows he will need) and give up more equity in the first round, the venture capitalist holds onto the money until the entrepreneur comes back for second-round financing.

The corporate entrepreneur will probably underestimate his or her needs for other reasons. One is that few corporate entrepreneurs understand the costs of running a business—the supplies, rent, and other costs. Many have never had to produce a budget, and even those who have have never been penalized if they went over budget. A second reason is that, not having traded equity for capital, the corporate entrepreneur will probably not be as cost-conscious.

The other reason to have a contingency allowance is that

successful investments cost more to bring to completion than do failures, and the corporate venturists, working in an environment where failure has been the norm, may very well find themselves surprised by the amount of success they are generating. It would reflect badly on the new-venture business management to run out of funds as many of the ventures started were successfully reaching milestones and getting close to becoming successful new businesses.

Invest 20 Percent Annually

The final rule of thumb is to try to become fully invested (leaving ample margin for future-phase financing and contingencies) in four to six years. The new-venture business almost invariably finds itself in a dilemma at this point. After six years, venture groups may be pushing the limits of their corporate lifespans if they have not made enough initial investments. Since it takes the average corporate venture seven years to reach a profitable state, the venture group wants to arrive at the end of a 12- or 15-year life with a minimum of ventures in midstream.

On the other hand, it makes no sense to jump in and commit the entire fund too early in its life. Unless good ideas are just floating around for the picking (and they rarely are), there is no reason to get into the venturing business with anything less than utmost caution.

There should be no pressure to perform quickly. If there is pressure, the program could be doomed to failure no matter what the venturists themselves do. If, on the other hand, care is taken and caution exercised, a corporate venturing program can be very promising.

Chapter Eleven

Oversight and Handholding

The final piece of the venturing puzzle involves monitoring—of both the venturing operation and each individual venture. There are three types of monitoring:

- Evaluative reporting
- Formal reviews
- Informal on-site communication with venture personnel

Monitoring the venturing operation is a corporate issue, and monitoring each venture can either be done centrally or by the venture organization as part of its fiduciary responsibility to the corporation.

Monitoring is the ongoing risk assessment and risk management process that goes on in any business situation—continually asking whether the venture or product is on track, and if not, why not, and how it can be brought back on track. Managers must use past experience to look for signs that something is wrong, checking actual results against planned projections, and drawing up plans for the future that take current reality into account, rather than perpetuating the assumptions of the past.

Monitoring entails an implicit commitment to the venture. There is no point in monitoring unless the company intends to help solve problems, rather than just disband the venture. Only when the problem cannot be controlled, as with technology- or market-related problems, must management deal immediately with the possibility of calling it quits.

Good guidelines, a clear strategy, and regular reporting are key ingredients for successful monitoring of the venturing operation. For individual ventures, the most important element is a well-documented business plan with clear goals and milestones, as well as tight financing and regular reporting.

Monitoring also assumes the existence of a data base. Since a good part of the information remains with the people involved in developing ventures, at least one of those people must be involved in the monitoring.

MONITORING THE VENTURING OPERATION

There are four basic criteria on which the venturing operation should be measured:

- The flow of ideas and prospects
- The quality of business analysis
- Relationships with the rest of the corporation and with the people in individual ventures
- Financial management

When evaluating the flow of ideas and prospects, management must note whether the venturing operation has set up a formal mechanism to collect ideas and a program to reach out into the corporation for those ideas. The group should continually be marketing this program to people in the company. The venturing operation should respond quickly to people with ideas, getting those ideas into the evaluation cycle, and taking initiative to get suitable projects moving in a timely fashion.

The quality of business analysis is sometimes hard to measure. In the venturing organization's later life, the quality and progress of funded proposals can serve as a measure of the quality of the business analysis initially used to select the projects, but in the early stages of venturing the group must be judged more on the thoroughness of its research and evaluation (which should be documented). If the group is constituted as an NBU, those to whom it presents analyses for decision making will be able to judge the quality of those analyses by how easy it is to make the resulting decisions.

The venturing team must maintain good relations with a number of people. They will need to turn to people at all levels in the corporation for ancillary support, as well as to build a network outside the corporation for proper screening and evaluation of ideas. Maintaining good relations with people who submit ideas is crucial; if people feel they are not being heard, ideas will dry up. Senior corporate officials, even after they have "bought into" the venturing idea, need to be kept well informed. The management teams of individual ventures are also important constituents of the venture team.

The venture team will be judged on its negotiating skills, both in negotiating with people in the corporation for things the venturing group needs, and in negotiating with entrepreneurs and venture managers over the terms of those operations.

As time goes on, these criteria will change in importance. For instance, the flow of ideas is critical until the venturing operation becomes fully invested (if the operation is constituted with a committed fund). If the venturing operation does not have its own fund, financial management may be more difficult, depending on the reporting arrangement and responsibilities.

The structure of the venturing operation determines whom it reports to and who will monitor it. In a new-venture division, the venturing team reports to the divisional CEO, who in turn reports to the corporate CEO. A new-venture group may report directly to the CEO or to a senior vice president. A new-business unit reports to the decision-making body with regard to new ventures.

There are two levels of monitoring for a division. The venturing group will be monitored by its immediate superiors, as would any department, except that the monitoring will be done according to the guidelines laid down in Chapter 5.

Actual monitoring of the venturing operation should be conducted by a new venture board, which will probably be a subcommittee of the company's executive committee. Formal reviews by this board should take place quarterly or at least semiannually, and there should be a less formal update more frequently.

MONITORING VENTURES

When a venture is formed, there are two types of monitoring organizations that need to be established. One is a group analogous to the board of directors of an independent company. In the new-venture group model this monitoring committee should consist of the venture's COO or general manager, one member of the venture group (preferably the person who did the initial evaluation of the venture), and executives from three or four of the company's operating units whose scope of work or activities has some connection to the venture's purpose. These outside directors must be willing to take part in all venture reviews.

The second monitoring function should be taken on by the venture-group individual who is on the board. This person will do the day-to-day monitoring, just as the individual venture capitalist who sits on the board of a venture does. The difference is that the person in the corporate setting is the fiduciary for the entire board, since all board members are from the same company.

These functions are the same in the venture-division model, except that the board is often made up of some people from the division within which the venturing team resides, and that there are fewer directors from other operating units of the parent corporation.

In the new-business unit model, the place of the venture-group board member is taken by the corporate executive most intimately involved in the process of putting together the business plan, recommending the venture to corporate decision makers, and shepherding its approval through. Since this venture "champion" executive probably has a number of other obligations, he or she will not be expected to put the time into monitoring that a new-venture group member would. Day-to-day contact should be taken on by one of the executive's line support people, probably the person involved with the detail work of the evaluation and approval process to begin with. The basis for venture continuity, the data base, will be entrusted to some extent with this staff person. Alternatively, this function may be delegated to the person in the new-business unit involved with the task force that evaluated the business plan.

One company, which used the ad-hoc venturing model, set up the following procedures:

> A board of directors for each venture "sets checkpoints tailored" to the venture "which, if exceeded, require review/approval" by the corporate executive committee (CEC). The board chairman is also given the responsibility of reporting to the CEC when "checkpoint limits are exceeded, as well as major changes in mission and plan variances."
>
> The chairman also has the responsibility to review the venture's performance annually with the CEC and provide "an assessment regarding continuation and an outlook for its integration" into the company mainstream. In explaining the changes, the company stated that "the changes demonstrated the intent to not over-manage or unnecessarily control" the ventures, rather "to assure that major variances surface in time for top management to take alternative actions if required."

Although this system is well intentioned, there are numerous problems in its implementation. The chairman, as well as board members, are division and corporate executives, usually serving on several boards at one time. When competitive pressures rise in their business areas, the resulting demands on their time could conflict with their involvement in the ventures.

According to the guidelines, board meetings were to be held quarterly, but only for two hours. Meetings started and ended on time, regardless of whether the agenda was complete. Board members rarely visited their ventures. Two ventures had their respective chairmen visit them once in three years. As one would expect, on these occasions the red carpet was rolled out, and the executives were given a carefully rehearsed program. There were never any other visits by corporate staff that would compare with an investor's visiting his start-up.

Reporting Procedures

Whatever the model, the board should meet regularly, with a formal report given by venture management at each meeting. More frequent informal updates can be given by the venture management to the day-to-day monitor.

The reporting procedure should be consistent and formalized so all ventures report in the same manner. At the first board meeting, the venture's chief operating officer should define the mission and objectives, making sure to clearly state any changes in the mission or objective from those in the original business plan. Then the COO should go through the current strategy for developing the mission and objectives, including the products and services involved, the prospective markets served, the technology, and a recap of the details of the first-year plan.

If any of these have changed significantly between the time the final version of the business plan was evaluated and the first board meeting, this should be stated clearly. Business plans do change, as entrepreneurs become more knowledgeable about the realities of the technology, market, and competition. The board must understand these new developments, and the business plan must be updated.

At this time, the milestones should be reviewed carefully, and any changes in conditions should be discussed in terms of how they might affect achievement of the milestones. The financial plan should be reviewed to make sure it conforms to the new, more realistic milestones. The administrative plan should also be reviewed. By this time, the entrepreneurs should know how closely their administrative procedures will resemble those of the company at large, and where they will diverge.

If these baselines are drawn clearly at the first meeting, the format for future meetings can concentrate on objectives. The board and monitors will be looking for variations between the plan and the actual results, why these deviations have taken place, what accomplishments have been attained, and whether the venture can be retracked and retimed for success or whether it is time to consider folding the tent. If the problems seem to be correctable, then a new plan should be drawn for the next review period, and the annual plan must be adjusted accordingly.

Beyond Paper

Corporations tend to have a paper-based reporting and monitoring process. This is not the way to handle venturing. Documents don't tell the whole story.

First, many executives don't read paper assessments closely enough to pick out the subtleties. They may not spot problems until they become trends based on a number of reports. The tendency is to spot something, go back to old reports and find the beginnings of the problem, then say "Why didn't I see this before?" Second, because the conditions of an entrepreneurial company change so fast, by the time a report is put on paper, the business may have already undergone a significant change.

Venturing demands ongoing, hands-on monitoring, either by a member of the new-venture group (if there is one) or by a senior executive intimately involved in the venture's birth. This hands-on management is the only way to feel the pulse of the venture, the only way to pick up the tone of voice with which venture management makes its reports.

A lot can be hidden in recitations of facts and numbers, either on paper or in a formal presentation. But far less can be hidden from an interested venturist or executive who wanders around the venture's facilities, talking to people and getting a sense of how things are progressing. Visual observation is the only way of maintaining a current sense of the health of the venture and having a basis for evaluation.

Only by probing can management get to the root of problems and their ultimate solutions. The written record must be probed. The venture management must be probed when it makes verbal presentations. And what the investors see as they wander around must be probed.

In one company, the monthly financial reports showed inventory building up. Everyone thought it consisted of parts or products waiting to be shipped. It took some serious questioning to get the venture management to admit that the product was just not selling.

In another instance, there was a backlog of orders, while inventory remained high. The venture monitors asked why the inventory was not being used to reduce the backlog. At the same time, the cost of goods was steadily rising because the vendor costs were going up, which threw a curve into the equation. The truth was that early units of the product had gone out with bad parts and had been returned and redone with "quick fixes." Unfortunately, these failed and the units were sent back again. The inventory consisted mostly of units that did not include a necessary engineering change, even though vendor costs included the costs of reengineering.

Monitoring is a combination of risk assessment and management. The reviewers look for problems in all major areas, assessing potential impacts and probabilities, and determining the best way to handle the problems. Sometimes these risks will become evident at formal review sessions. Often, the reviewers will have had hints of these risks during their less formal monitoring.

The areas to be monitored are the same as those addressed in the evaluation. They include

- Management
- Technology/product
- Market

Problems in any of these areas will have a financial impact on the venture. There are a number of symptoms of potential risk, underlying reasons why these symptoms appear, and remedial actions that can be taken.

Monitoring Management

The most obvious symptom of management problems is the failure to achieve milestones. Sometimes investors learn that they are getting false, misleading, or incomplete information from the management team to cover up delays and other problems. Although this is a clear sign of poor management, it is not usually known until things are already bad and the venture is in jeopardy. A third sign of management difficulties is low employee morale, perhaps even a large number of resignations or requests for transfer. Finally, project personnel should all be working with the same information base. If personnel are uninformed, and everyone seems to have a different story regarding the status of the venture, management problems are probably the cause.

One reason for these problems, assuming that the initial evaluation was correct and the project is feasible, is poor communication within the project team. Poor communication breeds problems in employee relationships and is often a sign of more basic management deficiencies.

Solutions range from asking the management team for a crisp definition of the problem, alternative solutions, and an action plan, to changing reporting relationships, changing management, or reevaluating the entire project on a sunk-cost basis.

Monitoring the Technology/Product

Some of the most frequent technical difficulties involve the technical milestones' being missed, performance problems in the product, product costs higher than projected, or the product's failure to meet specifications. Technical breakthroughs by other companies may make obsolete the planned approach.

The reasons for these difficulties can range from uncontrollable technical obstacles to factors such as too-tight specifications and overengineering, to a simple lack of discipline.

Although corrective actions may take the form of minor adjustments, they are more likely to involve major changes. Redesign may be needed to reduce manufacturing costs and customer price. Unyielding technology may force less ambitious technical objectives. Closer cost and technical controls can be exercised, and additional resources may be added. Experts can reevaluate the technology, and the project can be funded in smaller

increments to make sure it stays on track and stays monitored. To do this, near-term milestones should be established—a so-called measured-mile system. More drastic
actions include changing the technical management and
reevaluating the project as a whole, again, on a sunk-cost
basis.

Monitoring the Market

The two most frequent market risks encountered involve
announcements by competitors of similar products or
products that make the one being developed obsolete, and
low advance orders for the product in the absence of significant competition.

Reasons for these problems may include a misassess-
ment of the market, the wrong marketing strategy, a market that has slipped, unanticipated competing products, or
a project that is ahead of the marketplace. Periodic system-
atic reviews will provide indications of the scope and magnitude of these events.

The easiest response is to ask for a revised plan that takes
into account new realities and addresses the changed marketplace. Test markets can also be studied. The project can
be slowed down if it looks as if it is ahead of its time (it is
harder to speed it up). Or, the project can be reevaluated
in its totality, on a sunk-cost basis.

GETTING OUT

One of the options we have listed for each of the three
problem areas is reevaluation of the project as a whole.
And one option after that project has been reevaluated is
getting out.

One of the reasons venture capitalists are more success-ful than corporations is that they seem to know better when and why to get out of a project. Successful venture capital-ists project what can go wrong and how they will get out with a minimum loss.

Alternatives include selling the venture as an operating entity, either to another company or to the entrepreneurial principals. The technology can also be sold, but not the capital assets, or the venture can be merged with another company, most likely a competitor.

Companies vacillate about getting out of a venture. Con-flicting objectives, career paths, and corporate politics in-variably color decisions.

This was illustrated in one venture, in which consistent losses of 50 percent of gross revenues forced corporate management to install yet another general manager. With the instruction either to save the venture or kill it off, he proceeded to have the staff identify alternatives for im-proving the business. The venture had a significant posi-tion in two business areas and was on the verge of announcing significant entries in both areas. However, before any opportunities could be explored, he told the corporation that the venture could not be saved and rec-ommended termination. During the next four months, un-til the decision was formally announced, he took actions that increased costs and decimated the venture's critical technical capability. Soon after folding the venture, he as-sumed an executive position in another division.

Making the Decision

Picking winners is notoriously hard. Why to get out and when to get out is a judgment that is as subjective as the decision to invest in the first place. Most venture capitalists say the decision to get out comes "when it is hopeless," but the definition of hopeless is a hard one to make, and many have been burned.

The four major reasons for getting out of a venture include people problems, product delivery problems, continuous delays in meeting milestones, and technology that does not work.

By far the most frequent reason for getting out of a project relates to people problems. The dynamics of any group are hard to anticipate and possibly even harder to manage. If the team does not work well together, the whole venture will more often than not fall apart. People problems are the underlying reason for most of the other problems in any venture.

When a venture is being established, at the same time a plan is being formulated to integrate the venture into the fabric of the company, an alternative plan should spell out the ways to get out of the venture with a minimum of loss.

Although venture capitalists say there are really only three times to sell a company and get out with a limited loss—the start, the first sale, or first entering the black—corporations, because of the tax loss potential, are not as limited. While profit, or at least some cost recovery, is desirable, companies have other considerations. In the example of the company that sold off its two business areas to separate companies, its reputation was at stake. Not only was it in danger of leaving customers in the lurch, but there was also the question of whether customers would believe the company's commitments in the future. In this instance the company was clearly not motivated by financial gain, because the total price received did not begin to recover even a fraction of the operating losses.

Companies have more financial exposure than venture capitalists. Contractual arrangements between corporate ventures and vendors are often made on the strength of the parent company's backing. Often the company will have to buy out existing commitments to preserve its credibility. Reengineering costs and production-line modifications by the vendor can lead to substantial termination costs. Another option for companies is to integrate some of the venture's capabilities into existing or planned products that the company will market.

AFTERWORD

The internal venturing puzzle is large, with many irregularly shaped pieces. In order to make it work, a company must make a concerted effort. A large degree of cooperation and trust is required; corporate executives must believe that those who are running the new-venture business and all of the individual ventures have the best interests of the corporation at heart. Entrepreneurs and internal venturists must believe that the corporation is really trying to make venturing a success.

There are five truths about venturing in the corporate setting:

1. Venturing is different from running an established business. The degree of certainty in an established business is missing from the venture.

2. Venturing requires an integrated process that must be followed if it is to succeed. This process consists of a number of phases linked together. All steps must be performed from the time an idea is submitted up until and during commercialization.

3. Venturing will succeed only if the process is customized to fit a company's culture, value system, operating style, and organizational framework.

4. Venturing requires an unconditional commitment by company management.

5. Venturing has three main success factors: process, culture, and people. The process must be interwoven into the company's culture, with the appropriate people involved in the business of developing and managing new ventures.

We believe that if these five truths are kept in mind, companies will end up transferring more ventures into the corporate fabric than they do now, and throwing fewer onto the trash heap.

———

We invite thoughts, comments, and anecdotes about corporate venturing efforts—successful or not—or information about other corporate venturing approaches that have been used.

This information can be sent to:

Corporate Venturing
P.O. Box 1388
Bethesda, MD 20817

INDEX

Index

Index

Index

Markets
  business plan, marketing plan, 92–94
  monitoring, 195
Maturation levels
  immature v. mature businesses, v
  management style changes, 38
  new-venture group, 150
Milestones
  ad hoc venturing, 163
  oversight and hand-holding, 190
Monitoring
  assessing and running new business,
    44–45, 51
  new-business charter, relationship be-
    tween corporation and new busi-
    ness, 116–117
  new-business unit, 156
  oversight and hand-holding. *See* Over-
    sight and hand-holding
Morale
  failure of venture, effect, vii–viii
  protective internal corporate ventur-
    ing, 8
  venture shock, 122

New-business charter
  generally, 102
  commitment delineated, 103–104
  consistency, 105
  defined, 102–103
  duration of new-venture business, 108
  financing
    generally, 108–109
    financial management, 109–110
    long-term funding, 110
    managing, cost of, 111
  management and controls
    generally, 111
    active or passive management, 111–
      112
    conflict between management and
      new-venture people, 112–114
  objectives, 105–107, 112
  performance measurement

  generally, 114
  compensation, 114
  evaluation criteria, 114–115
  relationship between corporation and
    new business, 116–117
  suspension or termination of venture,
    115–116
New-business unit
  organizational options. *See* Organiza-
    tional options
  oversight and hand-holding, 186
  staffing, 164
New-venture division
  organizational options, 159–161
New-venture group
  organizational options. *See* Organiza-
    tional options

Objectives
  need for clearly defined, 6, 18–19, 25–
    26
  new-business charters, 105–107, 112
Older employees
  corporate entrepreneurs, 136
Operations
  business plan, operational plan, 94–96
Organizational options
  generally, 144–145
  ad hoc venturing, 161–163
  new-business unit
    generally, 151–153
    supporting venture, 156–159
    task force, 153
    tasks, 154–156
  new-venture division, 159–161
  new-venture group
    generally, 145–146
    composition, 147
    responsibilities, 148–149
    transfers, 149–151
    venture management, working with,
      149
  transferring new-venture group to es-
    tablished company, 159–161

Index

Index